LOVE LETTERS FROM A 20-SOMETHING

A Memoir in Essays About Becoming and the In-Between

Bella Scipione

Bella Scipione

DISCLAIMER / AUTHOR'S NOTE:
This book is a work of nonfiction. It reflects the author's memories, perceptions, and personal experiences. As memory is subjective and time alters perspective, some events have been reconstructed, condensed, or described from the author's point of view.

To protect privacy, some names, identifying details, and personal characteristics have been changed. In certain instances, individuals may be portrayed as composites, and timelines may be adjusted for narrative clarity. Any resemblance to persons living or deceased beyond those expressly identified is coincidental.

The views and opinions expressed in this book are the author's own and do not reflect those of any institution, organization, or employer with which the author is or has been affiliated.

In addition, this book is not intended as a substitute for professional medical, psychological, or mental-health advice. Readers are encouraged to seek appropriate professional support when needed.

ISBN-13: 9798218944643

Cover art by: Amanda England
Library of Congress Control Number: 2018675309
Printed in the United States of America

Dedicated to my family. I am not me, without you.

Bella Scipione

Table of Contents:

Introduction: A Love Letter to the Reader

Dear Reader,

I've always dreamed of writing a book. However, I thought it would come at a time later in my life when I had things a little bit more "figured out". I started a travel blog when I turned 22 during my first time backpacking across Europe with my sister, G. The blog began as a way to reflect on my own experiences, a memoir to the people and adventures I journeyed. It was through this blog that I uncovered parts of myself, as a 20-something, and as a writer, that the answers of what, or who, I was living for slowly began to reveal themselves.

For so many of us we expect our early twenties to come packaged neatly with answers set by certain milestones like a degree, a job, or a partner. Things that society (specifically Western society) tells us are checkpoints on the road to adulthood. Yet, my answers have always seemed to arrive unexpectedly: in a ferry terminal in Greece, where the missed departure felt like an invitation to slow down; in a Dublin pub, where laughter with friends made time stand still; in a tattoo shop tucked down a smoky alley in Naples, where permanence and impermanence blurred together; and in the quiet hum of Berlin's streets, where history whispered reminders of resilience.

This book is not a how-to guide for your twenties. I don't have a roadmap, and I'd be lying if I said I've figured it all out. What I do have are stories, snapshots of the moments that changed me, the heartbreaks that opened me, and the friendships that blossomed around me.

My blog has slowly turned into something more than just a journal. It has become a mirror, reflecting parts of myself I didn't know I was searching for. Writing down my experiences made me realize that life is less about the places we go and more about the connections we make with others, with ourselves, and with the moments we wish we could hold onto forever.

There's a quote that has stuck with me which I stumbled across while sitting in one of the many Parisian cafés during my hours of reflections: *"We write to taste life twice, in the moment and in retrospect"*. That's what this book is, a second tasting of life. It's a collection of love letters to the lessons I've learned, the people who shaped me, and the places that became a part of me.

This decade, and this life, are full of wonder and beauty even through its many contradictions: chasing freedom while longing for stability, finding yourself while getting lost in others, falling in love with the world while grieving what you've lost or left behind. These contradictions are what make our twenties so vibrant and painful, and so worth writing about.

This book is for anyone who has ever felt untethered, who has ever wondered if they're doing it right, or who has ever needed a reminder that the struggle is a part of your story. It's for the dreamers, the travelers, the seekers, and for the ones who haven't quite found their footing yet.

If you've ever fallen in love with a moment, if you've ever had to say goodbye to someone you weren't ready to let go of, then I think you'll find a piece of yourself in these pages.

This isn't a guidebook, and it's not a map. It's a love letter to my twenties, to the places I've been, and to you, wherever you may be on your journey.

With love,

Bella

Bella Scipione

Part One: Lessons in Love and Loss

Chapter 1: Grief is the Price We Pay for Love

Dear Reader,

There's a certain heaviness that comes with loving deeply, a quiet knowing that everything we hold close will one day slip from our grasp. Grief is the shadow of love—it follows, inevitable and unrelenting, in the wake of what we cherish most. As humans, we grieve many things. Loved ones who have passed, pieces of ourselves we have outgrown or abandoned, the presence of those still living but now distant, unreachable.

Yet, grief isn't just about endings, but also the spaces in between: the moments when you catch yourself feeling all of the energies that are no longer, the memories that echo in the silence, the way the world keeps moving even when yours feels like it's come to a standstill. We grieve moments we can never return to, words we never said, the weight of all that remains unfinished.

However, grief is not just sorrow, it is love persevering, both wound and remedy. It is proof that something, someone, some part of us mattered so deeply that its absence leaves a hollow in our hearts. And what a beautiful thing that is, to have loved, to have been, to have existed so fully that we now feel the ache of its absence.

This chapter isn't just about grief as a farewell; it's about the ways we learn to carry love forward, even when it changes form. Because if grief is the price we pay for love, then surely the depth of our sorrow speaks to the immensity of what we've had.

***

The first time I walked through the streets of London was with my sister, G. As lively and busy as the city was, it had an overwhelming sense of somberness, wrapped in an air of mourning. Just a week earlier, Queen Elizabeth had passed away, and her presence still lingered on billboards, shop windows, and makeshift flower memorials.

As we wandered through the historic streets, one phrase caught my eye, repeated over and over, beneath her portrait: "Grief is the price we pay for love."

The words struck something deep within me. Six months prior, I had lost a close college friend in a car accident. The grief still felt raw, surfacing unpredictably in moments I least expected. Seeing these words—spoken by a Queen but felt by so many—made me pause, pulling me into a space of self-reflection.

Queen Elizabeth had first spoken them in a message of condolence to the families of those lost in the 9/11 attacks. Now, they reappeared in the wake of her own passing, an acknowledgment of the collective sorrow of a nation grieving a monarch who had, in many ways, been a constant.

With each step through the streets, G and I's laughter from the night before, recounting our first encounter with British boys, faded into silence. The weight of the words settled in, and I found myself pondering the other side of grief, the one we often overlook: love. The two are inseparable, bound together like light and shadow. And in that moment, I began to understand that our sorrows are not just burdens to bear but proof of love that endures long after its presence has changed form.

Even though I was beginning to unveil the shadows of grief, I didn't fully feel it until we were halfway through our three-week backpacking trip in a small town in Greece, after missing a ferry by two minutes. That day marked exactly six months since MK had passed, and as the sun set in pink skies, I felt everything all at once.

G noticed. I had been irritable, the kind of irritated that doesn't come from missing a ferry or a long day of travel. She watched me, her brow furrowed, waiting for a moment to finally ask, "What's wrong?"

I hesitated, staring blankly at my phone as we silently ate our gelato under the stars. The words felt too heavy to speak, but the silence between us made them inevitable.

"Today's the six-month anniversary of MK," I said.

Understanding dawned in G's eyes, softening her gaze. She didn't need me to explain further because suddenly, my moodiness all seemed to make sense. We sat there, watching the sky darken, and let the silence fill the space.

I journaled that night, reflecting on the beautiful life of MK and her passion for life like no other. I wrote about how she lived every moment like it was her last and made the people around her feel loved, valued, and safe. It was then that I remembered that while it is important to mourn the lives of those we lose, it is also important to celebrate it—that double-edged coin of grief and love. And on that quiet evening in Greece, as the palm trees danced through the pink skies, I knew love had never left me.

It was a cold Thursday night in March, the kind where the air carried the persisting bite of a Midwest winter, but the promise of spring whispered around the distance. I had decided to stay in for the night, wrapped in the warmth of familiarity with one of my many lovers at the time.

The past two weekends had been a blur. Our twenty-something-person friend group had just returned from a wild, sun-drenched Senior spring break in Miami, followed by one of our infamous house parties for St. Patrick's Day. We were six weeks away from graduation, clinging to every moment, desperate to stretch our time just a little bit longer.

The house, usually pulsing with music and dancing, was quiet that night. It was just me, my lover, and the sound of us munching our way through the kitchen when the front door swung open.

In walked MK.

She was her usual, radiant self, cheeks flushed from the cold, eyes bright with mischief, a knowing smile stretched across her face. She had done what she did best. She had Irish-goodbyed from the bar, slipping away unnoticed and Ubering back to our place, her second home, to grab some of her things.

"I met the cutesttt guy tonight," she gushed, stretching out the word like she always did when she was excited, her voice laced with that infectious energy only she possessed.

I watched her as she rambled on about the boy she had just met at our college town bar, every word spilling out with unfiltered enthusiasm. That was MK—she talked about life the way most people talked about falling in love, with uncontainable joy and electricity that brought every room to life. There was a quirkiness to her, a magic that didn't need explaining, it just was.

At least three hugs and two "okay, I gotta go, my Uber's here, I love you's" later, she was at the door.

I can still see her now—the way she glanced back one last time, the way she existed so fully in that moment.

She shouted out one final, "Love you", as the door closed behind her.

Early the next morning, I woke up to footsteps thundering up the stairs of our three-story home. A familiar voice called out, frantic and trembling.

"Ruby! Ruby! Girls! Girls!"

I jolted awake, heart pounding. My mind scrambled to catch up.

I threw on a pair of sweatpants and cracked my door open.

It was Ruby's mom. She was breathless, her eyes wide and glassy, moving as if her body hadn't caught up with her panic. She started toward the next flight of stairs—toward Ruby's room.

"Mom? What's wrong?" Ruby's voice called from above, still groggy, but alarmed.

"There's been an accident," her mom said, her voice cracking mid-sentence. "I didn't know...I didn't know if you were in the car."

I stood frozen in the doorway.

"Wait—what happened?" Ruby asked, stepping down the stairs to meet her mom. "What are you talking about?"

Her mom turned toward her, relief and fear crashing together in her face. "You weren't answering your phone," she said, almost as if scolding her out of sheer desperation. "I didn't know. I didn't know if you were okay."

"I'm here, I'm okay," Ruby said gently, stepping forward to hug her. "I'm sorry. My phone was dead."

"You didn't answer," her mom repeated, still breathless, still trembling.

"I'm here. I'm okay," Ruby said again, firmer this time, her arms wrapped around her mom as if holding her together.

"There was a car accident," her mom said, barely above a whisper. "MK was in the car. She's at the hospital. Her mom's on her way down from Chicago."

I finally spoke. My voice quieter than I expected.

"Wait…what?"

I had just seen her, MK, less than eight hours ago. Still giggling, still lit up from her night out.

"Do you girls know how she got home last night?" Ruby's mom asked, glancing between us. "Was she with you?"

"Yeah, we were all out," my roommate Ruthie chimed in as we all tried to make sense of everything. "But MK left before the rest of us did."

"She came back here," I added. "She told me she was heading home, said her Uber was pulling up."

"She was in an Uber?" Her mom asked. "Are you sure?"

"That's what she told me," I said. "She looked at her phone like she got the notification, gave me a hug, said, 'Love you,' and walked out the front door."

13

But now it wasn't adding up.

MK had been admitted to the hospital as a Jane Doe. First responders hadn't found any ID at the scene—no wallet, no phone, nothing. Just the wreckage. It wasn't until they traced the plates on the car that they were able to identify her.

"They confirmed it was her by her license plate," Ruby's mom said. "It's MK."

Everything in me turned cold. My thoughts tangled, overlapping with disbelief.

Jane Doe. The words made my stomach turn. I hated that she was labeled that. MK was anything but a Jane Doe. She wasn't some anonymous figure, some unknown name.

She was loud and bright and beautiful. The kind of person you remembered after a single conversation. The kind of person who couldn't blend in if she tried. There was nothing "unknown" about her.

She said she Ubered. She told me. She hugged me. I watched her walk out.

Why would she lie? Or…did she? Why didn't I walk her out? Why didn't I double check? What if I'd just asked one more question?

A flood of what-ifs hit me all at once—every version of the night we could have had if something, anything, had gone just slightly differently.

Ruby, Ruthie, and I sprung into motion, calling the rest of our roommates: Aidan, Josie, and Isabelle, urging them to come home. We had no details, just a pit in our stomachs.

I dialed Stella and Eric, MK's roommates, also two of my best friends.

"Have you heard anything?" I asked, already knowing they hadn't. "Please come over. It's MK. She's at the hospital. We don't know anything yet."

I sent out a text to the rest of our twenty-person group chat:

"Hi guys. MK was in a really bad car accident last night and in the ICU right now. We don't have much information, but things are not looking good. We'll try and update as best we can. Her family is coming down now but keep her in your thoughts and prayers. Love everyone so much."

Within seconds, each person had sent out a heart to the message. It was 10:45 on a Friday morning, and it was clear that everyone felt the gravity of it immediately. There were no questions asked. Just silent acknowledgement. We all knew this was serious.

A few hours passed.

My roommates and I walked down to a nearby church. None of us were particularly religious anymore, but all of us were raised Catholic. And going to the church wasn't about belief, exactly. It was about presence. About being in a place where silence carried weight. Where we could sit still, together, with something bigger than our panic. It felt like the only place to go.

Back at the house, Ruby's mom came down with more information. I typed out another update to the group:

"MK's family has arrived and are with her now. It's going to be a tough next couple of days. We are hopeful, but at this point she is not improving."

"In the meantime, we ordered some margs from Mula and are planning on watching some basketball here. Anyone is welcome to come by if they need a distractor or some love."

It wasn't good news. But none of us were ready to give up hope. Not with MK.

We shifted into action. Creating a shared album of photos, printing them out, taping them across the post in the middle of our living space. It wasn't much, but it was something. It kept her with us—every smile, every goofy pose, every snapshot of her radiant, ridiculous self.

Mula margaritas and Creighton basketball were two of her favorite things. So that's what we leaned into. We set up the TV. Pulled out every spare chair. Mixed the drinks. We didn't know what else to do, except surround ourselves with pieces of her and wait for some sort of miracle.

One by one, everyone started arriving.

Our house—affectionately called *The Lot* because of the giant back space where we'd throw parties for our whole class—was always our gathering place. But this time, it wasn't loud. There was no music blasting or people shouting over pong tables.

This time, it was quiet. Reverent. A space to hold each other. To hold the hope.

That was the next 48 hours.

Twenty-something of us, MK's people, gathered in the only place that felt right. We listened to music, passed around eggs benedict and cartons of takeout, playing games, anything to keep our minds distracted. We took walks from my house to MK's, only a few blocks apart—routes she had walked dozens of times.

We spent our days, morning to night, in each other's company. School wasn't even a consideration. There were no classes. No deadlines. No projects. The only assignment that mattered was showing up for one another. And we did.

On the second day, still hoping—still waiting for any sign— Ruby's parents returned to the house. Only a few of us were there when they arrived: the housemates of The Lot, along with Stella and Eric. We were scattered around the living room—on the couch, the floor, curled into corners of chairs.

I was on the couch, clinging to Stella, my freshman-year roommate and one of the few people who knew how to hold me when I couldn't speak. I felt her heartbeat against mine, both of us still.

Ruby's mom stepped into the room. Her face told us everything before she even spoke. There was a long silence. We braced for whatever it was she had to say.

She looked at all of us with tears in her eyes, her voice steady.

"MK's mom has made the decision to move forward with MK's wishes to be an organ donor. There's no brain activity. MK is no longer with us."

The quiet cracked.

Crying filled the room. Not loud, or frantic, but deep and immediate. Tears ran freely. People folded into each other's arms. No one was sitting alone.

I didn't let go of Stella. She didn't let go of me. Our bodies, pressed close, radiated warmth that felt almost too much to hold—but still, we didn't move. We couldn't.

When we had somewhat collected ourselves, if you could even call it that, another text was sent to the group:

"We have an update. Please come to The Lot as soon as you can."

One by one, the rest of our friends piled in, filtering into the living room. They didn't need to be told. They could read it on our faces, feel it in the way the air had shifted. Something wasn't right. The energy was different.

People found places to sit and once everyone was there and the room fell still again, Ruby's mom stood at the front and repeated the news. Almost word for word.

I looked over at my friend, Molly. Tears started spilling down my cheeks again. Somehow, it wasn't any easier to hear the second time.

Molly is one of the strongest people I know. Steady, grounded, the one I've looked to more times than I can count for calm in the chaos.

But now she was sitting on the floor, her knees pulled into her chest, her face flushed red, eyes vacant. She didn't say a word. She just sat there, curled in on herself, quietly crying.

And somehow, seeing her break made it all the more real. It wasn't just grief anymore. It was the kind of sorrow that steals sound from a room. That leaves you staring at each other like maybe if you hold on long enough, you'll wake up.

But we weren't waking up. This was real. MK was gone.

She had left our house that Thursday night for a late-night Diet Coke from McDonald's—or at least, that's what we pieced together.

Her car was found crushed to the towering pole with the glowing golden arches. A drunk driver had slammed into her—going more than 40 miles over the speed limit.

The doctors said she was likely gone in that moment. That it happened fast. That she didn't suffer.

Somehow, those words were supposed to bring comfort. But nothing really could. Not when it was MK.

The news had begun to spread—discreetly at first, then all at once. Messages started pouring in. Friends, classmates, people who had only known her in passing. Everyone reaching out with condolences, with offers to help, with stunned words that all seemed to carry the same undertone: this doesn't feel real.

And how could it? We were seniors. Weeks away from graduation. Inches from starting our "real" lives—applying to jobs, finalizing grad school plans, dreaming up new cities and new beginnings. We were in the golden stretch, the part where everything is supposed to feel celebratory. Safe. Most of us had built something special in those years—a makeshift family, a rhythm of connection, a shared language of memories and late-night laughter. And now that bubble had burst. No one could quite process what our group was walking through.

So, we did what we knew how to do best.

We gathered.

We hosted a memorial at our house—a place most people already knew as The Lot. We printed out photos of MK, stringing them along the walls and pinning them to the kitchen cabinets. A poster board stood by the front door, inviting people to sign it or scribble down a memory—some silly, some heartfelt. A slideshow played on loop in the background, full of moments that captured exactly who she was: magnetic, unfiltered, full of life.

Dozens of familiar faces walked through our door. Some had known her well. Others had only crossed paths with her once or twice—maybe at a pregame, maybe dancing in the moonlight in our backyard. But they all came.

Because when you met MK—even for a moment—you remembered her.

In the midst of our heartbreak, we tried to channel her spirit. We urged everyone who showed up to take this moment—this unimaginable loss—and turn it into something.

We wanted people to hear it loud and clear: Tell someone you love them. Don't wait. Life is short, and fragile, and rarely goes as planned. Say the words. Make the call. Give the hug. Because if MK taught us anything, it's that love is meant to be loud. And joy is meant to be shared. And none of us are promised tomorrow.

I had lost people close to me before losing MK—grandparents, close family friends, lives that had faded with time or illness. I knew death was a part of life. That grief, loss, and mourning were universal experiences, stretching across time, culture, and geography. It was one of the many things that made us human.

And yet, despite its inevitability, every culture seemed to navigate it in its own way.

In Mexico, families gather each year for Día de los Muertos, the Day of the Dead. But it isn't a day of sorrow, but of celebration. Altars adorned with marigolds, photographs, and the favorite foods of the departed are placed in homes, inviting spirits back for one night to share in the joy of those living. How beautiful is it to believe that death doesn't sever love, but simply changes the way it exists?

In Ghana, elaborate fantasy coffins are carved into shapes that represent the passions of the deceased—an airplane for a pilot, a fish for a fisherman, a Bible for a devoted Christian. It's a way of honoring their story, ensuring that even in death, they are defined not by how they left the world, but by how they lived in it.

Then, there are the Balinese cremation ceremonies—Ngaben, they call it. A grand, almost theatrical send-off where music fills the air, towering funeral pyres are set ablaze, and families rejoice in the belief that their loved ones are not gone but transitioning to the next life. There is no wailing, no black clothing—only the conviction that death is not an end, but a transformation.

Even in the animal kingdom, mourning is instinctive. Elephants have been known to gather around the body of a fallen member, touching them gently with their trunks, hovering as if to say goodbye. Some return to the site days or even years later, running their trunks over the bones in quiet recognition. If even they understood the weight of loss, then surely grief was not just human—it was woven into the fabric of life itself.

I thought about all of this as I tried to understand my own grief.

Losing MK wasn't like losing my grandparents or family friends. There was no gradual fading, no chance to prepare. One moment she was standing in our kitchen, alive in every sense of the word, and the next, she was gone. It was sudden, violent, incomprehensible. There was no celebration, no ritual to soften the confusion, the what-ifs, the edges of sorrow—only an absence where she used to be.

And yet, in the days, weeks, and months that followed, my twenty-plus-person friend group—along with everyone who knew and adored MK—found her in every moment we could. We celebrated her in laughter, and in tears, that echoed loudly throughout our homes. We honored her through the songs she would sing and dance to, and in the one-liners that would forever only belong to her.

Today, we cling to her memory in the smallest things—a tequila ranch water, her favorite drink ordered at a bar, pictures and videos that beautifully capture her personality, a group chat where someone will type "MK would've loved this," and we'd all know, without question, that she is still with us.

I've made a promise to myself to honor her in the only way I know how—with time, with presence, and with people who knew her best. Every year, I make the trip to Chicago—MK's hometown, and now home to Stella and a few of our college roommates. It brings me comfort, being with them, the same way it did when we clung to each other in those early days.

Each of their homes has some kind of bright, vibrant tribute to her. A framed photo. A Polaroid clipped to a mirror. An empty bottle of 818 tequila repurposed as a flower vase. These things light up the room, the same way she did.

"It's been three years, but it also feels like ten," Ruby said one night while I was visiting.

"I still think about how every one of us showed up," Ruthie added. "We didn't leave each other's side. I don't think we could've gotten through it otherwise. None of it was easy but being together made it feel a little more possible. No one had to grieve alone."

"I just miss her so much," Josie said, her voice soft. "And I know her ass would love all the trends that have popped off since she's been gone."

The three of them still live together, along with our friend Liz, in a home MK would've absolutely adored.

It's beautiful. Lively. Full of color.

It will forever be hard to understand why she was taken from us—so young, so full of life, with so much more to give. Some losses just never make sense, no matter how much time passes. And yet, when you look through history, through stories and songs and all the people who left too soon, you start to notice a pattern. Some people—the extra luminous ones, the ones who burn brighter than most—just don't stay long.

Maybe that's part of the mystery. Maybe their purpose isn't to grow old, but to leave something behind that time can't touch. A spark. In the fullness of youth that echoes in the people who loved them.

Whatever that's all about, I don't think we'll ever fully understand. But I do know this, her absence is undeniable. But so is her presence in all the spaces she once filled.

And so, we carry her forward in the only way we know how. Not in silence, but in joy. Not in forgetting, but in remembering. Not just in mourning, but in love. And if you, too, have lost someone, you can do the same. Yes, cry. Mourn. Be angry. Be confused. Sit in the sorrow when it comes—because grief deserves to be felt. It needs to be felt.

Grief doesn't care about timing. It doesn't ask permission. It shows up in waves—unexpected, uninvited. At a stoplight. In a song. While folding laundry. It catches you off guard and leaves you breathless.

There is no one way to grieve, no perfect blueprint for healing.

It's a process—nonlinear and deeply personal. Some people find comfort in saying their loved one's name out loud every day. Others hold their memories quietly, like sacred keepsakes, tucked into the folds of daily life. Neither is more right. Both are full of love.

But I do believe this: it is always important to celebrate. To laugh again. To dance again. To live in a way that honors the ones we've lost. Not just with sadness, but with presence. Not just with tears, but with intention. Because the love doesn't go away when someone is gone. It just changes form. And if grief really is the price we pay for love, then how we carry that love forward is a choice. And we should choose to carry it in joy.

Chapter 2: The People We Loved Before We Knew Ourselves

Dear Reader,

Love in our twenties often feels like both a beginning and an unraveling. It's raw, exhilarating, and sometimes heartbreaking. We stumble into it with wide eyes, believing that every connection might be "the" connection, the forever. But as time passes, we begin to see that love isn't just about who we meet—it's about who we become because of them.

Love stretches us, shapes us, and sometimes shatters us, only to reveal parts of ourselves we might not have discovered otherwise.

We live in a time where moving on isn't as simple as saying goodbye. Social media makes sure of that. We watch people from our past move forward in real time—new partners, new homes, and new lives. Their updates pop up when we least expect it, pulling us back into memories we thought we'd outgrown. However, there's some beauty in that. This serves as a reminder that growth doesn't happen in isolation. The people we once loved are part of our story, just as we are part of theirs.

This chapter is for the ones who stayed too long, for the heartbreaks that taught us boundaries, and for the romances that felt like universes in themselves. It's for the lessons learned in quiet heartbreaks and loud goodbyes, for the nights spent wondering if love was supposed to hurt this much, and the mornings we realized we deserved more.

Because love isn't just about finding the right person. It's about finding yourself—sometimes through them, sometimes after them.

✳✳✳

Part I: Madison

There's an illusion of permanence that we attach to relationships when we're young and in love—a belief that the intensity of our feelings will somehow anchor people to us forever. We think that because we feel deeply, the connection will endure, unshaken by change. We build futures in our minds, ignoring the inevitability of a life that is constantly shifting.

This illusion makes it hard to let go. We convince ourselves that closure comes from a final conversation, a neatly tied ending where both people walk away with clarity and peace. Yet, I have rarely seen this to be true. Closure isn't something someone gives you, but something you create within yourself when you stop looking for answers in someone else. Real closure arrives in the acceptance that not every story needs a concluding chapter to be complete.

I struggled with this concept of closure, this illusion of permanence, in most of my adult relationships. I'm a romantic, a believer in true love, in soulmates. I love deeply—so deeply, in fact, that I have the words "Amore duro", meaning "love hard" in Italian, tattooed on my right bicep. Growing up as a ballerina, I'd sit on stage in my slippers and tights, wide-eyed and enchanted, watching *The Nutcracker* year after year. I was captivated by Clara, saved time and time again by the Nutcracker Prince, their story a recurring promise that love was always meant to be magical and everlasting.

But outside of the fairytale, I was lucky enough to witness love in its truest form. My parents were the perfect personification of true love. They were engaged within six weeks of knowing each other, married a year later, and then, nine months after that, I arrived. Just recently, they celebrated twenty-six years of marriage, and their love has only deepened over time. They have set the standard for what a trusting, communicative, loving, and understanding relationship looks like.

Their love is built on mutual respect and unwavering support. They have shown me that true love is not just passion and fairytale endings but partnership, patience, and the choice to love each other every day. Watching them, I've learned that love isn't just about the beginning—it's about the commitment to keep choosing one another through every phase of life.

However, knowing this, I still struggled. I sought love that mirrored their devotion, but I often found myself chasing intensity rather than stability. I confused passion with permanence, thinking that the right love would always feel exhilarating instead of steady. But my parents' love has taught me that real love isn't about the highs and lows—it's about the consistency, the still moments, and the belief that you are always in it together.

My first real relationship was everything all at once—exhilarating and passionate, but also overwhelming and suffocating. His name was Caleb and we met when I was 18, standing at a bus stop in Cabo San Lucas, Mexico, the summer before I left for college. It was a connection that hit fast and hard, one that felt cinematic in the moment but chaotic in hindsight. We fell into each other quickly, maybe too quickly. It was a whirlwind that left me dizzy, lost and confused.

For a long time, I tucked it away as nothing more than a summer fling. One of those stories you tell your friends with a shrug—half romantic, half ridiculous. A subplot.

So, when he messaged me out of the blue three years later, I was more amused than anything.

"Hey shawty, you in Denver? I'm driving through tonight. Let's catch up."

First of all, "Shawty"? Really? I remember staring at my phone, half-laughing, half-cringing. Who even says that anymore? And who did he think he was, calling me that like no time had passed?

I rolled my eyes and instantly thought back to Cabo. We were so young. I never really took him seriously then, and I definitely wasn't about to now—especially after a message like that.

"Lol, yeah 'shawty'. I actually am in Denver. I'm down," I replied.

We made plans to meet at Top Golf that night. Public place, low pressure. Worst case scenario, at least I'd get to hit a few golf balls and call it an experience. He mentioned he was with a friend, so I quickly texted my best friend Lindsey and asked her to come with me. I definitely needed her as my wing woman.

Lindsey and I arrived early to scope things out and grab a drink before the guys got there. We posted up at the bar, ordered something with just enough tequila to take the edge off, and tried to play it cool. But I was anything but calm. My heart was racing.

I glanced down at my Apple Watch:113 bpm. Nearly 40 beats higher than my usual resting heart rate. Great.

"I think I'm gonna pass out," I half-joked, clutching my drink.

Lindsey raised an eyebrow and smirked. "Babe, you've got this. You look hot. Worst case scenario, we drink, hit balls, and leave with a funny story."

She was right. She always is.

When the guys finally walked in, I felt a jolt of recognition that surprised me. He looked different—older, obviously—but also more confident. More at ease in his own skin. And when he saw me, he didn't hesitate. He walked right up and gave me this big, familiar hug, like he'd seen me every day for the past three years. There was something disarming about it.

And when we all were comfortable and started talking, I remembered.

He was funny. Like, actually funny. The kind that catches you off guard and makes you laugh out loud. He had that same charm I remembered from Mexico, but now it was grounded in something a little more grown.

I felt the butterflies immediately. That fluttery, nervous-excited feeling you get when someone completely captivates you. I wasn't expecting to like him this much. But there it was.

I really, really liked this guy.

There was something about our energy together—like magnets being pulled. It was electric. Intoxicating. A connection that makes everything else blur around the edges. I'd never felt anything like it, and it completely consumed me.

After a few hours of Top Golf, none of us were ready for the night to end. We hopped from bar to bar, driving all over Denver until someone threw out the idea of Boulder—and, in that classic twenty-something spirit, we all just… said yes. Why not? His friend offered to be DD for the night, and Lindsey (ever the trooper) took the passenger seat. I knew she wasn't into the friend, not even a little, but she stuck it out with no complaints.

Caleb and I tucked into the backseat, completely wrapped in each other. Since leaving Top Golf, we couldn't let go. Holding hands, leaning into each other, our knees bumping as the car wove through city streets and hit the open highway.

The windows were rolled down, the night air loud and fast as we flew down the 75-mph stretch toward Boulder. I handed him my phone and opened my Spotify playlists, nervously waiting for his reaction—because everyone knows, your music taste is your personality laid bare.

He scrolled, nodded, then broke into a grin.

"These are some *hot tracks,*" he said, glancing over at me. "Such a vibe."

The music thumped against the wind, filling the car with a soundtrack that felt like the first scene of something bigger. This was the beginning of our story, and I felt it in my bones.

We spent the night and next morning together. No distractions, no bar noise, no crowd, no alcohol blurring the lines. Just the two of us, catching up. Telling stories and asking questions, filling in the gaps between the version of us that had existed in Mexico and who we were now.

And we got deep fast. Peeling back all the layers of our lives.

"This feels insane to say out loud, but I really like you," I said, voice steady but heart pounding. "And it's kind of freaking me out."

He didn't flinch.

"It's not insane," he replied without missing a beat. "I feel it too."

The next night, we went on another date. And from that moment on, we were in it. We talked and texted every single day. I returned to Omaha to finish my semester, and he started his new job in Madison, Wisconsin, just a five-hour drive away, which felt closer than it should have. We were close enough to make it work. Close enough to try to at least.

Within two weeks, he flew out to Omaha to visit. I introduced him to all my friends as we welcomed the start of summer— drinks on rooftops, party buses, early May nights that welcomed Summer.

For months, we lived in a rhythm of movement. Back and forth between each other's cities. Meeting each other's people. Going to parties, music festivals, weekend trips. We weaved our lives together in this kind of fast-forward montage, as if we were doing everything we could to make up for lost time.

And every moment with him felt perfect. He was spontaneous, passionate, and unapologetically intense. I was so drawn to him.

It was a constant rush of adrenaline, of attention, of wanting to know what would come next. I didn't know it at the time, but I had become addicted to that feeling—the high of it all. The thrill of being chosen, wanted. Of being wrapped up in something that felt just out of control enough to be exciting.

But the thing was—when we were together, it really was perfect, effortless. Like we were in our own little world. But when we were apart, it was a completely different story. Toxic. Unstable. Painful in ways I didn't know how to explain.

And maybe the hardest part was that I was never really allowed to call him my boyfriend. We were so infatuated with one another, saying "I love you" early on. But when I'd ask, time and time again, "When are you going to ask me to be your girlfriend?", he'd say, "Bella, I love you. But why do we need to put a label on things?"

"Well, are you seeing other people?" I'd respond.

I already knew the answer. I had his location. I had the gut feeling. But I didn't want to admit it to myself—not yet. So, I played into his same game. Tried to beat him at it.

"I'm going on a date tonight," I told him once, lying through my teeth just to get a reaction.

"Why do you have to act like that? I know that's not the truth."

It always ended in fights—fights that started to feel like their own kind of intimacy. The push and pull. The tension. The making up. It was exhausting. But I had confused the chaos for passion. The hurt for intensity.

One night, the fear of losing him swallowed me whole. We had gotten into another argument, and I was convinced it was over. I got in my car and drove to Madison without telling him—four and a half hours of white-knuckle anxiety and emo music on full blast.

As I pulled up to his place, I saw him. He was standing in the doorway, holding hands with a blonde girl.

My breath caught. I froze. Do I get out now? Do I make a scene? Do I drive away? I waited. Watched. He walked her to her car, still holding her hand, then kissed her through the driver's side window before turning to head back inside.

My blood boiled. My whole body shook. I turned off the car. Walked straight in—he'd left the door open.

"Who the fuck was that?" I asked, steady but shaking.

"What the fuck?" he said, startled. "What are you doing here?"

"Who the fuck was that?" I said again.

He stammered. "It was nobody. Just… a random girl I've hooked up with before. I thought you were mad at me. I didn't know what to do. I invited her over." His eyes filled with tears. "I fucked up. I'm so sorry. I'm so sorry."

And just like that, I folded. He knew exactly how to pull me back in. The crying. The apologizing. The self-loathing that felt like remorse but was probably just guilt.

I hugged him. Told him it was okay. Apologized to him. For what? I still don't know. But that moment—the way I soothed him while bleeding inside—marked something in me. I had become so accustomed to the toxicity, the game of cat and mouse, that I started to believe it was normal. That love was supposed to feel like this.

I forgave him, over and over again. The same fights would play on loop but still, I kept going back. Kept hoping the next time would be different. That *he* would be different.

The final straw came that fall, during a trip to Nashville over fall break. It was one of our final trips that all twenty-something of us were in attendance for. By this point he had found his way into our group. My friends adored him. Probably because I never shared all the dramas and harsh realities of the true dynamic of our relationship. I didn't want to say out loud the kind of partner he really was, not wanting to admit it to my friends, but more importantly not wanting to admit it to myself.

On the first night of the trip, something in me felt off. It was a feeling I couldn't shake, no matter how hard I tried to talk myself out of. Caleb was asleep next to me, and I picked up his phone.

I unlocked it, going through it, searching for my name in his messages. Nothing. I searched the word *"girlfriend."* And there it was.

A message to one of his best friends that sunk my heart into my stomach:

"Bro, this isn't easy having two girlfriends at once, but I kinda love it."

What. The. Fuck. I kept reading, my eyes scanning and body shaking.

"Katie's in Chicago right now, and I'm in Nashville with Bella."

Katie. I searched the name—nothing saved under Katie. But then I found the texts where he was calling someone Katie, saved under the contact, "Devin." I looked up my own number. I wasn't saved under "Bella," or even something generic like "B." I was saved under "Matt S". He had disguised us both under guy names.

My whole body went hot. Every cell in me screamed. I shook him awake.

"What the fuck is this?" I shouted, shoving the phone toward him.

His eyes blinked open, confused for a second, then panicked. I don't remember what he said first—probably tried to lie, then backpedaled, then apologized, like always. But I didn't care anymore. I had officially hit my limit.

I lost it, completely lost it.

We finished the Nashville trip as if everything was okay. I played it cool around the group, didn't want to ruin the trip for anyone else. But inside, something in me had finally snapped back into place.

A line had been drawn. And while I didn't say it out loud, I knew I was done.

In the weeks that followed, I kept asking myself:

Why was I so obsessed with someone I knew wasn't right for me? Why did I keep going back?

We watch our friends fall into those same dynamics—every part of us wanting to shake them awake from the daydream they're trapped in. But the truth is: no one can take the love goggles off for you. You have to be ready to see clearly. You have to *want* to. And even more than that, you have to be willing to look inward—to ask yourself what made that kind of love feel so intoxicating in the first place.

It took time for me to name what I had been through. To stop blaming myself for being "dramatic" or "too sensitive," and start calling it what it was.

Because the truth is—this is what dating a narcissist looks like. Being consumed by the highs, addicted to the validation, constantly chasing a version of love that's always out of reach. Narcissistic relationships thrive on imbalance. They keep you tethered through grand gestures followed by sudden distance. You know deep down that something isn't right, but you don't want to believe it. You convince yourself that maybe you're the exception—that your love, your loyalty, your sacrifice will be enough to change them.

That kind of love changes you. It rewires what you think is normal, and for a long time, it shaped how I approached love moving forward.

Now, even years later, I sometimes catch myself comparing new partners to him—chasing that same feeling he used to ignite in me. The thrill, the spark. I loved who I was with him or at least, I thought I did. There was always some new adventure, some wild plot twist. I longed for that kind of magic again.

But what I eventually realized was: those moments weren't magic because of him. They were magical because of me. Because of how I showed up in the world, curious, bold, alive. The spontaneity, the adventure, the energy... none of that was ever about him. It was always me.

The thrill I had been chasing all along wasn't him, it was me. Me, fully immersed in life, unafraid of what was next. And that? That's something I never needed another person to give me. For the first time in years, I wasn't reaching for someone else to save me. I was learning to save myself. That lesson—born from heartbreak and hard truth—became the foundation for everything that came next. Because when I finally stopped searching for love in the places that broke me, I found it in the most unexpected one: the world itself.

***

Part II: Rome

A year after cutting off Caleb for good, I had graduated from college and was gearing up for my first backpacking trip through Europe with G. Neither of us had ever been overseas before— nor had we ever spent much time alone together as adults. We planned out our dream itinerary, eager to romanticize and reclaim everything that had once felt like it belonged to someone else.

But nothing could have prepared us for the reality of living those dreams—the sheer vastness of the world, the joy of the small moments, and the way strangers can shape your story in just a single evening.

By the time we reached Rome, our motherland, it was our fourth stop. Ten days in, we had already been cracked open by experience, and we were actively evolving. Our inside jokes had doubled, our stamina had been tested. And somewhere between train stations and tiny coffees, we had started to find something that felt like freedom.

We had begun forming opinions about the people we met along the way—the Brits, Aussies, Canadians, French, Italians. Each encounter teaching us something new. Making us laugh. Making us think.

One evening, as G and I climbed the stairs to our hostel's rooftop bar, we were met with the familiar flutter of nerves. No matter how long I've been traveling, that little social anxiety never fully goes away. Entering a new hostel always feels like a dance—scanning the space, picking up the vibes, figuring out who seems open, who might make a good story, who feels safe.

And the stereotypes? They always show up. The Scandinavian who suddenly becomes the life of the party after a few drinks. The two Brits inexplicably arguing over their favorite football teams in the corner. The Southern Europeans, leaning against the balcony railing, lazily rolling cigarettes with thick accents and even thicker charm.

"Hey girls, lovely night, innit?" A voice said, full of ease and warmth. We turned to see a grinning British guy with raised eyebrows and a beer in hand.

"Once yous get your drinks, come and sit with our little group over there." He motioned to a long table, already buzzing with conversation and clinking glasses. His name was Syd. And he'd clearly been there for a few days—long enough to establish his own little micro-community. A makeshift crew of travelers gathered around card games and stories, all gearing up for a night out in Rome.

G and I got our drinks, exchanged a glance, and walked over. Among Syd's group, I locked eyes with a tall, green-eyed brunette with a mullet in a white-collared shirt. Feeling confident, I pulled up a chair next to him and introduced myself.

"Oi, what's doin'?", he said casually, "I'm Olly".

Another Aussie. *Great,* I thought to myself. G and I hadn't exactly had the best of luck with Aussie boys during our previous stop in Athens, but I wasn't about to let that stop me from sitting next to someone who was, quite literally, my type to a tee.

Olly and I hit it off immediately. Within minutes, he was teasing me about being American—specifically, the kind of American who spends spring break in Miami. To him, I was a walking stereotype, and he was absolutely delighted by it.

"You really went to *Miami?*" He laughed, mock horror in his voice. "You're like… every movie about American college girls rolled into one."

I laughed too, fully leaning into the bit. He was charming, quick-witted, and even when the jokes were at my expense, I didn't mind. There was something easy about him. Playful.

But then he noticed the tattoo on my left wrist. His smile settled as he reached for my hand.

"What's that mean?" He asked, turning my wrist gently in his.

"It's my friend MK's initials," I said. "She passed away a few months ago."

He softened. The playful glint in his eyes gave way to something gentler. Without letting go, he turned his own left wrist toward me. "This one's for my best mate, Cooper," he said quietly. "He died a few years back."

In that moment, the teasing fell away. We weren't strangers anymore. We were two people who understood loss—who carried it with us, not as weight, but as a reminder of the people we loved.

After that, our connection deepened. The conversation, once flirty and sarcastic, began to stretch into something richer. We made fun of each other's accents, sure, but we also talked about the people we missed, the things that shaped us, the parts of our lives that led us to the current moment.

And by the time the night was in full swing, it felt like we had known each other for years. We belted out karaoke in our hostel's bar. We stumbled through cobblestone streets with greasy 3 a.m. pizza slices in hand. We kissed under streetlamps that hummed with warm yellow light.

It all felt cinematic. But if I'm being honest, I thought that would be the end of it. A perfect one-night travel romance that had lived out its full duration. But, boy, was I wrong.

The next day, G and I were posted up at a corner table of a bustling little trattoria sat near the infamous Colosseum, indulging in yet another round of pizza. We giggled over last night's escapades like it was already ancient history.

"Do you think he remembers anything?" I asked between bites, still laughing.

"Honestly, probably not," G said, taking a sip of her red wine. "He was absolutely *blind* by the end of the night."

Blind was a term G and I picked up on that Olly and other Aussies we'd met loved to say, meaning they were so drunk, so "blind" that they couldn't even see.

And just as I lifted my glass to toast to our second day of Roman freedom, I saw Olly walk through the door.

"Oh my god," I said, smiling through my teeth, looking at Olly. "He's coming this way."

G turned back. There he was. Same mischievous smirk, same swagger in his steps from the night before. No warning. No text. Just... there.

"Oi, girls," he grinned, already pulling up a chair to our very *not three-person table.*

The waiter passed by, giving us a questioning look: *Who the hell is this guy? Are you good?* I gave him a smile and a slight nod: *Yes, we know he's a lot. And yes, we're good.*

Olly dove into the conversation as if he'd been there the whole time, his legs straddled around the chair, catching us up on his day like we'd asked him to. And somehow, despite his arrogance—or maybe because of it—it was charming.

"So," he said after taking a sip of my wine, "I'm heading to the Amalfi Coast tomorrow. Got three of my mates flying into Naples. What are you twos up to?"

G and I blinked at each other. *No way.*

"We're actually headed there too," I said, surprised. "That was already our plan."

Olly lit up. "Ah really? Sweet. Let's go together."

We didn't need convincing. Half the magic of backpacking is letting things unfold like this—unplanned, unpredictable, and a little bit wild.

That night was another blur of scooters weaving through Rome's ancient streets and an unshakable sense that adventure was just beginning. And by morning, we were on our train to Naples, ready for whatever the Amalfi Coast had in store.

The train ride is one of those memories I'll carry with me forever. I was in the window seat. Olly sat beside me, his head resting on my shoulder, our fingers interlocked together. For the first time since we'd met, things were still. The motion of the train was steady and smooth, a contrast to the past 48 hours.

We had shared a lot in that short time—jokes, stories, late-night pizza—but music was the thing that felt the most intimate. It had become a language between us. A way of saying what neither of us knew how to articulate. We each had an AirPod in one ear, taking turns choosing songs. No talking, just letting the music do the work.

Music has always been my way in. My memory keeper. My emotional compass. I've never been able to separate a season of life from its soundtrack. Every chapter I've lived plays in the background with its own score—songs that immediately anchor me to people, places, versions of myself I'd almost forgotten.

That train ride became a chapter all its own. The southern Italian countryside blurring past, the sun casting streaks of light across our faces, our shared playlist playing in our ears. Just us, music, and peace.

We had only one night in Naples, but with our restless Aussie travel companion, Olly made sure we made the most of our twelve hours. First stop: Pompeii.

At first, I resisted. After a long day of travel, all I wanted was bed and pizza. But Olly was insistent, and somewhere between my eyerolls and dragging my feet, I gave in.

Walking through Pompeii changed my whole mood. It was staggering. The way the city, once lavish and full of life, had been frozen beneath a blanket of ash after Mount Vesuvius erupted.

Villas, mosaics, amphitheaters—all preserved, standing as eerie monuments to lives interrupted mid-story. It was both haunting and beautiful, a strange collision of devastation and wonder. Sometimes, the things you resist most end up unforgettable.

The night called for rest, but "quiet" wasn't in an Australian's vocabulary. After inhaling massive pies of Neapolitan pizza, we decided, impulsively, to get matching tattoos.

It wasn't a totally new idea. We'd joked about it in Rome, but now it was real with one rule: it had to mean something. Not cheesy and not regrettable.

The shop was tucked in a sketchy alley, reached by a dead-bolted door and three flights of smoke-choked stairs. Inside: no tattoo chair, just four pool tables, a crowd of teenage boys slamming Peronis, and our silent guide who muttered that the artist was on his way.

Olly paced, torn between symbols and words. We'd agreed on a triangle—a sign of overcoming challenges. But suddenly, he wavered.

"I don't know if I want that," Olly said suddenly, mid-pacing.

"What?" I blinked at him. "Are you serious?"

He shrugged. "Yeah, nah."

My face flushed.

"You're kidding, right?"

"Nah."

Heat climbed my neck. I went first anyway. Five minutes later, a small triangle marked my ribcage—a symbol of connection that instantly felt like a solo story.

It wasn't the tattoo that stung so much as the embarrassment and disappointment. I'd let myself believe that someone like Olly, someone who blew in and out of places like a gust of wind, could follow through on something permanent.

I've always found that disappointment is the hardest emotion for me to sit with. Anger I can process. Sadness I can name. But disappointment? That one trails. It settles in your chest like something unfinished. Heavy, and quiet.

Growing up, love in my house was constant and encouragement came easy. We were celebrated, seen, supported. When we messed up, we were called in with compassion, not shamed. Our parents didn't yell or slam doors. They didn't belittle or threaten.

No, disappointment in our house came differently. It came in silence. In the quiet that followed a poor decision. In the look on their faces when they knew we knew better. That kind of stillness cuts deeper than any raised voice ever could. It forces you to sit in the discomfort of your own choices, knowing you let someone down—not because they're mad, but because they expected more from you. Because they know you.

And that stuck with me. Still does. Even now, when someone lets me down, it creases my trust in ways I can't fully smooth out.

It's funny how something as small as a triangle can say so much. A monument to a moment I hoped would be shared, and instead, ended alone. A reminder that expectation is risky when someone's never promised you certainty.

Looking back, it was naïve to expect so much from someone I'd known only four days. There was still so much we didn't know about each other. Still, when I feel a connection, I dive right in. I believe in possibilities. And when it turns out differently, the disappointment cuts deep.

To Olly's credit, a tattoo is permanent. I understood his hesitation—it wasn't about the ink itself, but the way it all unfolded. The buildup. The excitement. The sudden change.

Don't tell someone you'll do something meaningful with them, then back out the moment they commit. That's what hurt. Not the damned triangle, but the disconnect between his words and his actions.

We thanked the artist and left, the smoke hanging in the air. Out through the alleyway we went, kicking through the same scattered trash, and back into the streets of Naples. I walked ahead of Olly and G in silence, knowing I seemed dramatic. Maybe I was. But inside, I was just feeling the sting of disappointment—the ache of realizing something that had felt special no longer did.

I woke up the next morning still feeling a little off, but Olly didn't let me dwell on it. He apologized, made me laugh, and soon we were back to normal. The three of us checked out of our hostel, backpacks on, and walked to the Naples station to meet his Aussie mates—Callan, Dane, and Michael.

The boys arrived still drunk, riding the tail end of a bender. I remember standing by the metal turnstile as the three of them stumbled through loud, disheveled, and clearly dragged with frenzy. Olly's face lit up the moment he saw them. They were all grins, thrilled to finally meet the "two American sisters" he'd been hyping since Rome.

The hour-and-seventeen-minute train ride to Sorrento gave me a moment to breathe—and to catch up on my blog, updating family and friends who had been following along. G and I sat across from each other, pretending we didn't know the boys while the Italian natives around us shot them disapproving glances. The boys were loud, laughing and passing around a ten-euro bottle of vodka…at ten in the morning.

When we arrived, the station was quiet and nearly empty—no taxis, no signs, no clear way to reach our hostel in Positano. Just the six of us standing in the heat, sweating under our backpacks. A Korean traveler nearby kept pacing, glancing at us, then finally approached with his phone.

"Uh… are you going to Positano too?" He asked in clear but careful English.

"Yes!" G replied, relieved.

He smiled. "I think…maybe no bus? Italy system, not very clear, huh?"

We laughed. "You're telling us."

Back in Naples, I'd impulsively bought two bottles of wine—a decision that quickly proved brilliant. Two hours later, stranded and sunburned, those bottles became our saving grace.

Eventually we reached a local taxi service, and when the van finally arrived, we piled in: four Australians, two Americans, and one very patient South Korean. The whole scene felt like the start of a bad joke. I pulled out my phone to film the chaos: sun blazing, everyone packed in like sardines, sweat and laughter filling the van.

The caption read: "Four Aussies, two Americans, and a Korean walk into a van…" A living, breathing travel meme barreling toward the Amalfi coast.

As the van climbed the narrow cliff roads, conversation faded into stunned silence. The view unfolded in layers with pastel houses cascading down the cliffs, the sea glimmering below like crushed sapphire, sunlight bouncing off terracotta rooftops. It didn't look real.

Our days in Positano blurred together with its endless stone steps, salt and lemon in the air, and sunsets that dissolved into the sea. We boated to Capri, dove into turquoise water, wandered streets draped in bougainvillea. At night, we dance in a disco carved into a seaside cave, where music echoed off ancient rock.

That's where I met Alex—a radiant, free-spirited man from Mexico City. We clicked instantly, dancing and laughing under neon lights. At one point he turned to me and said, "You know, love is freedom."

My eyes widened, and I clapped once before shooting both pointer fingers into the air. "Yes!" I said, as if he'd just delivered some kind of revelation.

He was right. Love *is* freedom. It's the space to be fully yourself, to live with presence and intention. Maybe that's why everything with Olly felt so heightened. The places we were experiencing together made us softer, bolder, freer. We weren't ourselves there; we were movie versions untethered, and alive.

We laughed and argued, small things revealing how different we were. I'm slow to worry; Olly is urgency personified. His restlessness pulled me into moments I might have missed otherwise, and I loved that about him.

One afternoon, after too many Peronis, we stumbled into a jewelry shop. On a whim, he bought me a ring. As we walked back to meet our friends, who were waiting for the bus, he grinned, dropped to one knee, and asked, "Will you marry me?"

"Yeah," I said deadpan, as if it happened every Tuesday.

The crowd around us erupted in cheers. Strangers clapped and snapped photos, convinced they'd just witnessed a real Amalfi Coast proposal. It was completely unserious but somehow perfect.

That's what the trip had become: spontaneous, ridiculous, and deeply meaningful underneath it all. By the end, goodbyes felt heavy. Olly reminded me what it was like to fall in love again— not just with someone, but with life itself. Even fleeting love can leave the deepest imprint.

Bella Scipione

But what I thought would be a passing summer fling turned into something I couldn't have imagined. After Italy, Olly and I kept talking nearly every day. Not romantic, but as friends. A check-in here, a memory there, messages sent across time zones.

Before we even left Positano, G and I had made a promise: we'd visit the boys in Sydney. Over lunch in Capri, eating food we couldn't afford and pouring cheap vodka into fancy water glasses, we said it out loud: "We're coming to Australia." And we meant it.

A few months later, G and I followed through by working extra shifts, saving every spare dollar, and eventually boarding a plane to Sydney. Seeing the boys again felt surreal, like the continuation of a story we thought had ended. The same laughter, the same craziness, just on the other side of the world.

But as time had passed, so did our lives. Olly was in a new relationship, and the closeness we once shared vanished almost overnight. He kept his distance, barely speaking to me, then pulling me back in whenever things with his girlfriend fell apart— only to push me away again when they reconciled. It was a confusing, painful dance that repeated itself for weeks. And by the time we flew home, I knew that whatever version of us had existed in Italy was gone.

When the trip ended and life settled back into its rhythm, Olly apologized for all the drama that had occurred while G and I were there. I forgave him and we stayed in touch. A month after my return, I told him I'd been accepted into a master's program in London—a city he'd always dreamed of. A year later, he messaged me to say he was moving there too. That's when he asked if I wanted to travel through Europe with him that Summer.

Ecstatic, I said yes. My mind flashed back to Italy, to trains and music and possibility. We planned a three-week trip through the South of France and Northern Italy.

A week before he left Sydney, he called.

"Oh, by the way, we're traveling just as friends," he said, casually.

Sure, I thought. *Friends.* How could we spend three weeks together, back where it all began, and keep things strictly platonic? I shrugged it off, joked about it with my friends, and agreed without realizing he was completely serious.

He flew into London and stayed with me for a few days before we set off. Jet-lagged, anxious, and still the same persistent, intense Olly, he woke me up at 4:30 in the morning. "Come on," he said, "Let's ride bikes for the sunrise."

I thought he was kidding. I had been out drinking with friends the day before and the last thing on my mind was dragging myself onto a bike before the sun was even up. But he wouldn't let it go.

So, I threw on some warm clothes, rolled my eyes, and followed him out the door. He handed me one of his AirPods. "So we can listen together," he said.

The first song came on: *RÜFÜS DU SOL*—*Next to Me.* Those opening piano notes pierced our ears—*bing, bing, bing, bing*—and suddenly I was back on that train to Naples.

"And when the lights come down, I wanna feel you standing next to me..."

There we were, pedaling through the still-sleeping streets of London, the air sharp against our faces. The sky just starting to blush pink, our wheels humming over empty roads.

"And can you hear me out, there's a lifetime in front of me..."

Everything came rushing back. I was hungover, cold, and overwhelmed by a feeling I hadn't been prepared for.

"And when my time runs out, I wanna feel you standing next to me..."

This was *my* city. One of my favorite places on Earth. And now I was here, in the middle of it, at five am, watching the sunrise with someone who was so much more than just a friend in my eyes.

That night, I broke down to my friends. "I can't do this," I told them, "I don't know how to travel with someone who's been such a big part of my life and pretend it's nothing." But still, I steadied myself. Whatever happened, I'd be okay.

We set off for Marseille. On the flight, Olly held my hand the whole way, once again, sharing AirPods, our playlists looping like nostalgia. Then, as we landed, I saw a message pop up on his phone. It was him laughing with a girl back home about my meltdown from the night before. My stomach twisted. Just hours ago, he'd held my hand; now I was the punchline.

For a moment, I was furious. Then, like always, I told myself to get over it. To be easy, chill, unbothered. But even with the ache sitting in my chest, the week that followed was incredible—a blur of coastline, music, and motion.

We road-tripped through the South of France like we were in our own indie film with the windows down, music up, and sun pouring through the car. Town by town, we let the map lead us: Marseille, Toulon, Aix-en-Provence, Montpellier, Cannes—each one more intoxicating than the last.

Marseille was raw and magnetic, a city where the sea crashes against centuries of history. We explored the La Grotte Cosquer Méditerranée, a replica of a prehistoric cave buried beneath the Mediterranean. Horses, bison, seals were etched by hands 30,000 years ago. It was humbling being there, realizing that even then, people felt the same pull we do to leave something behind. To say, *I was here.*

Toulon was sleepier. We ate ice cream by the harbor, browsed a dusty bookstore, and let the tranquility fill in the spaces between us. Along the way, we swam in waterfalls, climbed rocky coves, and dove into water so clear it felt like glass. Our legs ached, our hair stayed salty, our skin turned bronze. Everything about it felt unpolished, wild, and effortlessly beautiful.

Then came Cannes.

That morning, Olly looked up from his phone. "Do you mind if we do our own thing today?"

"Sure," I agreed, grateful for a little space.

But by evening, I still hadn't heard from him. My phone was dying, and he had the only key to our Airbnb. When he finally walked in, he said it like it was nothing:

"I'm going on a date. Matched with a girl on an app."

I broke down again.

I knew we were "just friends." I knew he was single and owed me nothing. And I had respected that, despite everything we had shared over the last two years. But even friends don't do this. I had to draw a line not because I hated him, but because I needed to love myself enough to stop bleeding for someone who couldn't even hand me a Band-Aid.

That night, while he was off wherever, with whoever, I messaged him.

"I think I need to go my own way."

His response came instantly:

"Are you serious? What's your problem?"

"I don't want to get into this over text," **I wrote.** "I just need to do what's best for me."

The next morning, I sat outside the Airbnb with my bags packed. I didn't want a scene. I just wanted to leave. But then he pulled up, slammed the car door, and stormed toward me.

"Come upstairs. We need to talk."

47

Inside, it unraveled fast. His voice rose, hands moving in angry bursts as he shoved things into his bag. He was pacing, frantic.

"Will you just get over it?" He shouted. "We're never going to happen. You are the most selfish, immature person I've ever met. Everyone's laughing at you, mate. Who do you think you are? You have no idea how much stress you've caused me."

I backed toward the door, heart pounding.

"You said you wanted to talk," I said calmly. "But you're yelling. Step back and lower your voice."

For a second, he stopped. Then it escalated again—the yelling, the blame, the names. And I just stood there, letting his words fall but refusing to let them stick. I'd seen this before: the rage, the gaslighting, the twisting until you doubt your own truth. Not again.

I grabbed my bag and turned to leave.

He caught my arm.

"Don't you ever touch me," my voice low, firm. I yanked my arm away and walked out. Down the stairs, and into the street.

My phone buzzed nonstop—"You're selfish. You're immature. Come back." But I didn't stop. Didn't respond.

I found a bench near a bus stop, dropped my bags, and exhaled. I did what I had to do. I cut off all contact, this time for good. I didn't look back. The rest of my two-week trip, I traveled solo, finally certain I could handle whatever came next.

With time and distance, reflection sharpened into clarity. One truth eventually settled in: part of why our story felt so intense— so epic, so all-consuming—was because, for much of it, we weren't entirely sober. There were substances involved, both of us swept up in the fast pace of travel and the easy indulgence that follows you from hostel to hostel.

I hadn't realized it in Italy, but when I visited Olly in Sydney months later, I saw the struggle up close. Sobriety wasn't just an idea; it was a daily battle. I became one of his biggest advocates, encouraging him to stay clean as he prepared to move to London. By the time he arrived, he'd been six months sober, determined to rebuild his life. So of course, his memory of us—his version of what Italy meant—would feel different. I see that now.

Maybe that's something we don't talk about enough: what it means to love someone in recovery. There's a dissonance between who they were, who they're trying to become, and the space you hold in between. You start mistaking love for responsibility, thinking you can be their calm, their anchor. But you can't love someone into healing; they must choose that. And you must choose yourself, too.

When I look back on Olly and me, yes—I remember the turbulence and the hurt. But what stays isn't the devastation; it's the joy. The laughter. The moments that were pure bliss. Some of the greatest love stories end in heartbreak. That doesn't make them any less real.

I still wear the ring he gave me in Positano. I still think of him when *RÜFÜS DU SOL* comes on. That part doesn't just disappear.

It's like what my friend Alex once told me in that disco carved into the cliffs of Positano: "Love is freedom."

It took me a long time to understand what that meant—that some people aren't meant to stay, no matter how deeply we feel for them. We build illusions of permanence around temporary moments, convinced that if something burns brightly enough, it will last. But love doesn't work that way.

Some stories are told in years. Others in weeks. The difference isn't in their length—it's in their imprint.

For a long time, I carried both Caleb and Olly's absence like a wound, reopening it every time I thought about what could have been. I used to think that if it had been real, it wouldn't have ended. I don't believe that anymore. Sometimes love fades not because it was false, but because it belonged to a specific time and place.

Now, I see that the magic wasn't in the promise of forever—it was in how we allowed ourselves to live fully in the moment. That was the gift.

Because love's worth isn't measured by how long it lasts. Like my parents' love, it is present, patient, and kind. It is a steady commitment to growth, not just passion.

For years, I chased love like it was the missing piece of my story, now I know it isn't something to possess. It's something to experience for as long as it's meant to last. And sometimes, the greatest love story of all is the one we write for ourselves.

Chapter 3: Protect Your Peace

Dear Reader,

In the whirlwind of our daily lives, it's easy to become entangled in external demands, often neglecting the sanctuary of our inner calm. Our lives unfold in chapters of endless self-discovery through seasons of growth, reflection, and transformation. These shape how we connect with our core values, passions, and sense of independence. We often embark on these journeys alongside others, but there must always be a delicate balance between shared experiences and personal tranquility. True fulfillment comes not just from the connections we build, but from the peace we cultivate within ourselves.

"Protecting your peace" has become a mantra in my life, a gentle reminder of the importance of nurturing our inner serenity amidst the chaos of the world. For me, it signifies cultivating a heart that is calm and centered, regardless of external circumstances. It's about recognizing the energy we allow into our lives and understanding that we are the architects of our own reality. It means setting boundaries without guilt, walking away from what no longer serves us, and choosing to invest in the people and experiences that align with our highest selves.

This chapter invites you to explore what protecting your peace means to you. Energy is everything—it radiates from those around us and has the power to create magic or drain us entirely. We are the creators of our universe, and the power of attraction lies in how we envision ourselves in the world. When we learn to stand firm in our own energy, to release what disrupts our equilibrium, we unlock the ability to live with intention, clarity, and unshakable confidence.

So as you turn these pages, I encourage you to reflect on the spaces you inhabit, the relationships you nurture, and the boundaries you uphold. What do you need to let go of? What kind of peace are you seeking? And most importantly, how will you protect it?

***

My grandfather is the first person who comes to mind when I think of the word present. Robert (Bob) A. Scipione was born in

July 1937 in Brooklyn, New York, to Roman-Italian immigrants, Sabina and Dominick. To arrive in America at that time was to be born into a world in transition just as one era was fading and another was bracing to begin. His childhood unfolded in the long shadow of the Great Depression and on the eve of a world war. In those days, frugality wasn't a virtue—it was a necessity. Life was modest. Bread was baked at home, tomato sauce simmered on the stove, and its scent drifted through open windows.

For over 30 years, he worked as a biochemist, teaching at both the university and high school levels. My grandfather was a simple yet deeply complex man who spent his life reading and reciting poetry, playing piano, and delighting in what he called "exquisite" food and wine. He moved through life both effortlessly and intentionally, as if he'd discovered some secret rhythm the rest of us hadn't quite learned to follow.

He stayed on the East Coast with my Grandma Mary for most of my childhood, so visits were rare and usually reserved for the holidays. From what I remember, and what I've been told by those who loved her, my grandmother was an extraordinary woman. Though she was ill for much of her adult life, she lived peacefully and gracefully as a passionate cook and wonderful conversationalist. To this day, she remains one of the longest-living kidney transplant recipients on record. Much of that, we believe, was due to my grandfather's love, brilliance and unwavering dedication. He secured funding to conduct research on her transplant and worked closely with her doctors —giving her the gift of time. Decades, in fact that she might not have had otherwise.

Growing up, my siblings and I were taught many lessons: treat others the way we wished to be treated, stay curious, and show respect to all, especially our elders. But when you're young, those lessons feel more like chores than wisdom. After holiday meals, when the plates had been scraped clean and the table was littered with espresso cups, breadcrumbs, and the faint trace of garlic in the air, the adults would settle in. That's when time seemed to slow, and I'd find myself anchored beside my grandfather at the table, wishing I were anywhere else.

He'd lean back in his chair, swirling the last drops of red wine in his glass, and begin to speak in his measured, melodic cadence.

"You know, Dominick, if you don't read, you'll remain a wart on a log forever." He said once to my younger brother, Dom—completely serious, his eyes twinkling with conviction.

Dom absolutely adored Grandpa Bob. The two of them were close. Dom was always trying to pick Grandpa's brain about the philosophies of life, eager to hear his thoughts on Socrates, Plato, and everything in between. He'd ask ontological questions like, "Was there ever a time when nothing existed?" And Grandpa, without missing a beat, would dive right in.

Before they grew close, though, dinner table conversations were a different story. They usually consisted of Grandpa talking while we—mostly me, being the oldest—sat nodding half-heartedly, pretending to listen. My fingers would itch toward my phone on the kitchen counter. My knee bounced beneath the table. The seconds stretched endlessly. I was fifteen and impatient, preoccupied with the buzz of texts left unread and the vague dread of school on Monday.

But as I got older and less tethered to the noise of the world I was living in, I began to lean in. I started to see those conversations for what they were—gifts. Looking back, they were sacred moments disguised as ordinary ones: his voice mingling with the smell of coffee, the soft clink of cutlery, the low hum of the dishwasher starting its cycle. I didn't know it then, but what I was really learning wasn't just respect or patience—it was how to be *present*. The very thing he embodied.

Five years after my Grandma Mary passed, Grandpa moved out to Denver to be closer to us. Sunday dinners with him became customary, and trips to Washington Park, where he lived, became more frequent. My siblings and I would stop at Five Guys

Burgers & Fries beforehand, picking up a hot dog and milkshake for him, and join him for a picnic.

"Oh, this is just the best hot dog I've ever had," he'd say right on cue after the first bite of his Nathan's hot dog. "I can't remember the last time I had a hot dog like this."

We'd giggle, sitting in the grass, looking up at him perched on the park bench, napkin tucked neatly into his shirt collar. He said this *every* time we brought him Five Guys. Surely it must have reminded him of home—of Brooklyn in the Summer, maybe, when the scent of hot dogs intermixed with the sound of stickball in the street and radios crackling from open apartment windows.

Our picnics in the park remain some of my fondest memories with my grandfather. I can still see him—sitting upright on the bench, hot dog wrapper crinkled beside him, eyes gently closed as the breeze rolled across his face. The trees swayed above us, casting shifting shadows on the grass, and the sounds of the park hung lightly in the background.

After a few quiet minutes, he'd open his eyes and without warning, begin to recite:

"*A Bird came down the Walk*—"

"*He did not know I saw*—"

His voice was low but clear, full of reverence, like he was letting us in on a secret. I'd glance at my siblings to see if they were paying attention too. We never knew what poem he'd choose, but he always had one ready as if it were tucked in his mind like a favorite tune. And somehow, it always fit the moment perfectly.

Watching my grandfather—whether sitting quietly on a park bench, reciting Dickinson with his eyes half-closed, or savoring a hot dog like it was the finest thing he'd ever eaten—I realize now that he didn't need a formula to find peace. He lived it. He embodied presence not through discipline or ritual, but through attention. He paid attention to small things, and in doing so, taught us how to live with intention, curiosity, and grace.

Which brings me here. In a world overflowing with self-help books, wellness podcasts, and mindfulness trends, it seems like everyone has a formula for protecting your peace. There's no shortage of advice on what to do—meditate, journal, set boundaries, detox from social media. And while these practices can be powerful, I've come to believe that peace is deeply personal. It isn't something you can adopt from a checklist. It's something you define for yourself, based on what truly allows you to feel grounded, whole, and in control of your own energy.

So instead of turning to the so-called experts, I turned to the people I trust the most—my closest friends and family. I asked them how they protect their peace, and their answers were as varied and unique as they are. Some found peace in movement— working out, cooking, cleaning, turning stress into something productive. Others emphasized the power of boundaries: saying no, being mindful of what drains them, and shifting their attention when their energy felt depleted.

For some, protecting their peace meant simply disengaging by minding their own business, stepping away from negativity, and choosing gratitude instead. It meant making space for stillness, being okay with not being happy all the time, and allowing themselves the solitude to recharge—whether through journaling, meditation, or moments alone in the car. Others leaned into creative expression: painting, writing, even crying when they needed to, and letting emotions move through them instead of staying bottled up.

Then there were those who found peace in how they spoke to themselves. Two friends told me they're learning to catch their own negative thoughts when their mind whispers, *"You're not doing enough,"* they pause and replace it with something kinder, something true. Another friend shared the power of trusting her gut—how she often knows within minutes of meeting someone whether the energy is right, and how no longer forcing connections has brought her more peace than she ever expected.

What struck me most was that, despite how different everyone's approach was, all of them had one essential thing in common: they required *presence*. The ability to slow down, pay attention, and tune in—to your energy, your needs, and the signals your body or spirit are giving you. Protecting your peace, it turns out, isn't about doing more; it's about noticing more.

The irony is children do this instinctively. They live *in* the moment without even trying.

While I was still searching for a job in my field, I started working as a substitute teacher. I figured it would be temporary— something flexible and meaningful to do in the meantime. What I didn't expect was that it would be one of the hardest jobs I've ever done. By 10 a.m., my patience would already be wearing thin. By 2 p.m., I had a newfound respect for every parent, teacher, and daycare provider I've ever met.

But even in the midst of it all, I found myself quietly amazed. Children, for all their noise and unpredictability, are masters of presence. They wake up excited for what's in front of them, not burdened by what happened yesterday or anxious about what's to come. They find joy in things adults don't even notice—a pencil that sparkles, a dandelion growing through concrete, a cloud shaped like a dinosaur eating a marshmallow.

One morning during circle time, I asked the class, "What's your favorite month of the year?" A second grader raised her hand enthusiastically and shouted, "Fridays!" I smiled and started to correct her—but then I stopped. Because honestly? Same.

Children don't think in rigid timelines. They don't break life into quarters or seasons. They respond to what feels good, what lights them up. They don't multitask. They don't perform. When they play, they are all in. When they love, they do so without hesitation or expectation. They are proof that presence is our natural state but somewhere along the way, adulthood teaches us to forget.

We become restless, distracted, more concerned with what's happening elsewhere than with what's right in front of us. We start measuring time instead of living in it, filling empty spaces with noise, as if silence itself is something to escape. The very presence we once lived in so effortlessly becomes something we take for granted until one day, we realize just how much we miss it.

In a world that thrives on urgency, stillness often feels unnatural. We are conditioned to believe that peace is something to be *earned*—something we'll finally achieve once we fix everything, once we reach a certain milestone, once the frenzy settles.

But peace does not wait for perfect conditions. It isn't found in the absence of hardship, but in the way we move through it— with grace, with presence, and sometimes, with nothing more than the courage to keep going.

I didn't fully understand this until I moved to London.

I arrived bright-eyed and ready to take on whatever challenges came my way. How hard could it really be? I was independent, resilient—a woman who had spent the past year exploring corners of the world I once only dreamed of. I was stepping into a master's program surrounded by like-minded peers, and making friends had never been an issue for me before.

I was nervous, sure—but mostly excited, ready to welcome this next chapter.

Then reality hit. Hard and fast.

My flight had been delayed for weeks due to visa issues, and by the time I landed, I had just two days before classes began. I had no stable housing, no familiar faces waiting for me, and I'd missed orientation—the critical window when people form first impressions and friendships. The city I had been so eager to embrace now felt vast and indifferent.

I spent my first two weeks jumping from hostels to hotels, dragging five oversized suitcases behind me. Each one felt heavier with every move—not just physically, but emotionally. I had packed up my entire life, but I had no idea where I was supposed to *live* it.

Around day three, I found myself sitting on the curb outside my hostel, hunched over my phone, crying so hard I could barely speak. I FaceTimed my older brother, Christian. My chest was tight. My breath came in short, uneven bursts.

"I don't know if I can do this," I sobbed. "I feel so helpless. This all feels like a mistake."

Christian, ever the honest, blunt older brother, didn't sugarcoat it. "Well," he said, half-smiling through the screen, "don't let Mom and Dad say I told you so. You're going to be fine, Lala."

But I didn't feel fine. I felt undone. Unmoored. Like the whole world was moving forward while I was stuck trailing behind.

Just then, the hostel doors swung open, and a group of staff stumbled out—drunk, giddy, loud with laughter. One of them spotted me on the sidewalk and shouted, "Aw, don't let a bad night get you down! Come out and drink with us!"

I wanted to scream. The last thing I wanted was to get drunk on a Tuesday night with strangers. I had class in the morning. I didn't want to *numb* what I was feeling I wanted to *understand* it. I wanted to know why I felt so out of place in a life I had chosen.

The night before, I'd checked out of another hotel, dragging my bags behind me like a metaphor I was too tired to appreciate. At 11 a.m., I sat alone at the hotel bar, ordered a bottle of wine, and opened my laptop—not to write anything profound, but because writing was the only thing that made me feel remotely in control. I wrote in my blog to anchor myself. To try and make sense of it all.

Later, I shared a piece of it on Instagram: "One week living in my new city. I'm sharing this in complete honesty and transparency—this has absolutely been one of the hardest weeks of my life..."

I didn't post it for pity. I shared it because I needed to feel connected. I needed someone—anyone—to see me. Vulnerability, I knew, often walked hand in hand with strength. And in that moment, I needed to feel both.

That was my rhythm for weeks—oscillating between brave and broken, grounded and spinning. I never felt steady for long.

In class, I felt even more alone. My peers looked settled, confident, like they belonged. I was too overwhelmed to be curious, too self-conscious to initiate conversation. I was frustrated that I hadn't come more prepared. Embarrassed that I couldn't just keep up. I wore resilience like armor, refusing to let anyone see how lost I felt underneath.

Still, giving up wasn't an option. This had been my choice. I had something to prove—not to anyone else, but to myself. But in my desperation to make it all work, I wasn't actually living any of it. I wasn't present. I was constantly searching—grasping for safety, for stability, for peace.

Then, something shifted—suddenly, without fanfare.

I was sitting alone in the common area during lunch, mindlessly scrolling through Facebook pages like *Flat shares in London*, eyes glazed from reading the same tired listings. I was halfway through a message to a potential flat mate when I heard a voice.

"Hey, mind if I sit here?"

I looked up. A girl from class—Kat—stood beside me with a boxed sandwich and a kind smile. I nodded and moved my laptop aside.

She sat across from me and asked, "So, where are you from?" Not out of obligation, but with genuine curiosity.

59

I told her about Colorado, the visa delays, the five suitcases, the missed orientation. She listened. She asked questions. She laughed. And for the first time in what felt like weeks—I laughed, too.

That hour changed something. It didn't fix everything. But something in me opened. I was reminded that I wasn't invisible. And that reminder was enough to pull me one step closer to myself.

From there, I began forcing myself to do the things that had always made me feel more grounded. I walked for miles across the city, letting movement untangle my thoughts. I hopped between free gym trials, searching for the right fit. I took myself out clubbing, letting the music and the noise and the lights remind me that I was alive—really alive—in one of the most vibrant cities in the world.

And gradually, I stopped closing off. I began making eye contact in class. Answering questions. Asking them back. Smiling more.

Little by little, I started to recognize myself again.

I found a gym I loved. I secured stable housing. I made friends— some of whom I now consider family. But the biggest shift wasn't external. It happened inside of me. I stopped waiting for my circumstances to settle, and I started choosing to *engage* with my life. To invest in it. To invest in *me*.

I started to notice the small things again.

I'd sit on the top deck of the red buses, forehead pressed lightly to the glass, watching the city rush past beneath me. Shopfronts blurred into bakeries, bookstores, flower stands. I wasn't rushing anywhere in particular—I was learning to *see* again. I was falling in love with a city that had once overwhelmed me.

Underground, on the tube, I became an observer. I watched the expressions of the people around me—some reading, others daydreaming, some with eyes closed in practiced calm. A few looked lost, glancing up at the map, clearly riding the line for the first time. We were all headed somewhere, sharing the same car, the same moment, without speaking a word.

I watched the leaves fall from the trees, the seasons slowly shifting. I sat in parks with a book or a coffee, letting the cold air sting my cheeks, the sun warm my skin. I was reminded of the way my grandfather used to sit—quiet, observant, wholly there.

The world, I've learned, tends to reflect back how we treat ourselves. And I was finally treating myself with care instead of criticism.

I let myself cry. A lot. I let myself sit in the stillness and discomfort. I stopped running from the parts of me that felt unsteady, and in doing that, I unknowingly gave myself the thing I had been avoiding all along: *peace*.

I used to think peace had to be earned—something I had to achieve or chase. But I've come to understand that peace isn't something we find. It's something we create. It's not waiting on the other side of perfection. It lives in the present moment—still, rooted, and always available, if we're willing to pause long enough to feel it.

Not long after things began to settle, I became close with a friend named Jason—someone I connected with easily and deeply, the kind of person who feels like an old friend the second you meet.

He lived just down the street from that hostel—the one with the chipped brick and fading green sign. The one where I once sat sobbing on the curb, convinced I had made the worst mistake of my life.

The first time I walked to his place from my new flat, I passed that same spot. I didn't realize where I was until I looked up— and suddenly, I saw her.

Me.

Shoulders hunched. Heart racing. Face streaked with tears. Sitting alone on a cold London curb, phone clutched in her hands.

I wanted to stop and sit beside her. I wanted to hug her. I wanted to say: *You don't know this yet, but it's going to get so much better. You're going to laugh again. You're going to find your people. You're going to walk by this place one day—stronger, lighter, and more yourself than you've ever been.* And I'd mean every word.

Because now, I understand something I didn't back then.

Peace isn't something that finds you once the storm has passed—it's something you learn to cultivate *while* you're still standing in the rain. It took breaking down on that curb to realize that peace isn't a destination. It's a relationship—with yourself, your environment, and your ability to stay grounded through it all.

And the truth is, peace looks different for everyone.

Each form of peace is deeply personal, shaped by our experiences, our needs, and our growth. For me, emotional peace is learning to hold space for your feelings without letting them consume you. It's allowing sadness to exist without fearing it will last forever. It's knowing that joy is not something you have to chase—it's something you can create, even in the smallest moments.

Mental peace is dimming the noise inside your own head. It's recognizing when your thoughts are spiraling and choosing to redirect them instead of being controlled by them. It's the shift from *"I'm not doing enough"* to *"I'm exactly where I need to be."*

Physical peace is listening to your body—honoring it, moving it, resting it. It's taking a long walk to clear your mind, stretching after a stressful day, or simply breathing deeply and intentionally. It's the understanding that your body holds onto stress, and that sometimes, peace is as simple as letting go of tension you didn't even realize you were holding.

Spiritual peace is trust. It's the ability to surrender, to let go of control and believe that life is unfolding as it should. It's the comfort of knowing that not everything needs an answer right now. It is stillness in the soul—even when the world around you is in motion.

But peace is not a one-size-fits-all concept. And with that truth comes a need to unlearn the misconceptions that often surround it.

Some believe that protecting your peace means avoiding discomfort altogether. But true peace is not avoidance—it's knowing you can sit with discomfort and still remain grounded.

Others assume peace means isolation. But peace isn't about cutting the world off. It's about learning how to exist within it, without letting it disrupt the sanctuary you're building inside yourself.

Before you can protect your peace, you have to know what loving yourself, respecting yourself, and trusting yourself *actually look like* in your life.

Because how can you tell what's disrupting your peace if you don't even know what it feels like to be fully you?

Protecting your peace is about *awareness*—of what energizes you, what drains you, what aligns with your values, and what chips away at them. It's the difference between discomfort that helps you grow and discomfort that makes you disappear.

When you know yourself, you start choosing differently. You recognize when something is making you question your worth. You set boundaries from confidence, not guilt. You stop shrinking to fit into places you were never meant to belong. Peace isn't about subtraction—it's about *clarity*. And choosing peace means choosing *you*.

My grandfather didn't chase peace—he lived it. He found it in poetry, in music, in sharing meals with people he loved. As children, we knew how to do this too. We followed joy

63

instinctively. We rested when we were tired. We cried when we needed to cry. Somewhere along the way, we forgot. But maybe protecting our peace is simply about remembering.

Maybe it's not about building walls but opening up to what matters most.

Maybe it's about slowing down enough to notice the sunlight, to breathe, to trust. Maybe it's about choosing ourselves—not selfishly, but *intentionally*—because we finally understand that our peace is worth protecting. And maybe the most powerful thing we can do is stop waiting for peace to arrive… and start becoming it.

Chapter 4: Beneath the Labels We Wear

Dear Reader,

We move through the world carrying the labels we've gathered along the way: daughter, sister, friend, partner, student, traveler. They help people place us, understand us, make sense of us. Sometimes they even help us make sense of ourselves. But the longer I live, the more I've realized that these labels are only introductions, never explanations.

They tell part of our story, but never the whole one.

For years, I believed I had to outrun the labels that felt too small or too heavy. I thought becoming myself meant stepping outside of everything I'd ever been called. But growing up has taught me something truer: our labels aren't there to confine us. They're there to give us somewhere to begin.

Because beneath each one is a depth we rarely slow down enough to notice— the nuances, contradictions, memories, and desires that shape who we are when no one is looking. The parts that don't fit neatly into anyone's expectations, including our own.

The world may ask us to choose one identity, but we are always many things at once. This chapter is an invitation to look a little closer at ourselves, at others, at the stories that live beneath the names we wear, and at the truth that identity is something we grow into, not something we simply inherit.

***

I've always believed everyone should work in the service industry at least once in their lives. The long hours, irregular schedules, and weekend rushes demand more than physical stamina, they test your emotional bandwidth. Whether you're front or back of house, you learn patience, empathy, collaboration, and resilience in ways you can't fully understand until you're in it. More than anything, it sharpens your ability to see the people, dynamics, moods, and needs of those you serve.

Whether you realize it or not, bartenders and servers are constant observers. We're trained to read you through fragments of body language, tone, and timing. In the service industry, you learn to anticipate needs before they're spoken, to sense when someone wants conversation and when they want quiet, to recognize stress hiding behind a smile or gratitude tucked into a simple nod.

People want to feel seen more than they want to be served. Beneath the small talk and surface-level interactions, we're all just looking for comfort, recognition, and a place to land after a long day. You see people at their best: generous, grateful, celebrating something or someone. And you see them at their worst: impatient, entitled, distracted, sometimes painfully unaware of the person standing on the other side of the exchange.

We, the ones behind the bar or balancing trays, learn to notice the little things. The way someone nervously stirs their drink before a first date has even begun. The tight-lipped tension between coworkers sipping cocktails in near silence. The subtle glances, the shaking hands, the smiles that don't quite reach the eyes. It's a front-row seat to human behavior and a reminder that everyone carries more than what they show.

What number date is table 25 on? Third? First? The nervous fidgeting and careful conversation suggest the latter, but the way they lean in closer, the lingering eye contact, hints at something more.

Then there's table 7: a mom and dad wrangling two toddlers who are more interested in playing in their fried rice than eating it. The parents exchange weary glances, but there's laughter beneath the exhaustion. Maybe she's also a painter, a runner, someone who dreams of mornings of solitude she hasn't had in years. Maybe he writes poetry on his phone while the kids nap, reflecting on all the lives he's lived before this one.

It's a game we all play—guessing the stories of the people we serve, filling in the blanks with the bits we observe. Life in the service industry reveals a truth we rarely pause to acknowledge: the labels we so often use to define ourselves and others blur inside a restaurant or bar. In their place, we see stories. We see humanity. We see people trying, loving, hoping, and coping.

But here's the part most guests never see: on the other side of the exchange, the people serving you often live some of the most interesting, unexpected lives you could imagine. Service industry workers carry stories just as rich, sometimes richer, than those seated at their tables. Many of us choose this work because it offers the rare freedom to build a life around passion.

Your bartender might be saving to backpack through Southeast Asia. Your server might be a comedian practicing new material on you without you even realizing it. Your line cook might be earning a graduate degree between double shifts. And the owner might be an artist whose work hangs on the walls where you sit.

Service work becomes the bridge that supports all those other dreams. Traveling the world, pursuing education, building creative careers, raising families, or simply carving out space to become who we're meant to be. Behind every plate served and every drink poured is a whole life unfolding.

My ten years in the service industry has taught me that, at the end of the day, we are all more than the labels attached to us. Just as the one being served is not only a "mother" or a "CEO," we are more than "your server" or "your bartender." We carry dreams, grief, ambition, joy, and entire worlds of our own just like you.

And some people, like my sister G, make a point of bringing that humanity right into the work itself.

When G began her first serving job, she didn't just want to clock in and clock out. She wanted to bring something intentional into a space most people treat as purely transactional. She wondered how she could add value to an experience that, for many, was just another Wednesday night dinner.

So, she got creative.

At the end of each meal, when she handed her guests the bill and a pen, she'd invite them to flip the receipt over and write down two things: one thing they were grateful for, and one thing she did well, or could improve on, for next time.

It was a small gesture. But like most small gestures, it had a big impact.

Gratitude is disarming. It eases people. And in a world where service workers are often overlooked or treated as background noise, G flipped the script. She made her role interactive, reflective, even communal. She wasn't just asking for feedback. She was inviting people, strangers, to pause for a moment and consider their own humanness.

That's who my sister is. She has this rare, radiant ability to see goodness everywhere she goes. Whether she's in a coffee shop, a gas station, or the chaos of a packed Sunday brunch rush, she carries a presence that reminds people to slow down, to look around, to remember what matters.

In asking her guests to name a piece of their own gratitude, she wasn't just making their night better, she was helping them access something they might've forgotten on their own.

And in return, they often gave her something deeply human.

Scrawled across the backs of receipts were pieces of their interior lives:

"I'm grateful for good company."

"For good friends."

"For my health."

"For a warm house to go home to every night."

"I'm grateful for kindness."

"For sunshine."

Short sentences. Small admissions. A glimpse into who they were, what they valued, what they needed.

Not what they did for work. Not how many children they had. Not how many houses they owned.

The labels were gone.

And what was left was just...people.

I think that's why travel affects me the way that it does. It disrupts the way we perform at home and makes room for other versions of ourselves to surface. Over the last few years, seeing the humanness in others, and in myself, has started to show up more frequently. It's an awareness that's snuck up on me. Like an unexpected shift in light. And really, probably just my frontal lobe starting to make its final close.

When G and I booked our three-week trip to Australia, we didn't exactly have a detailed itinerary. The plan, if you could even call it that, was simple: fly into Sydney, rent a car, and road trip up the eastern coast all the way to Cairns, the gateway to the Great Barrier Reef.

We were so caught up in working two jobs, scraping together enough money just to make the trip happen, that the logistics part...well, it fell by the wayside. There was no deep dive into travel blogs or packing guides. No thorough weather checks. Just seeing where vibes would take us.

So, imagine our surprise when, four days into the road trip, parked in a sleepy coastal town called Hervey Bay, we finally opened the weather app and learned a very important fact: Cairns in January is smack in the middle of wet season. As in, the kind of wet where the region gets up to 2,0000 mm of rain, nearly 80 inches, in just a few months.

We sat in a booth at a quaint little country club we'd stumbled into for lunch, staring at the weather app and then at each other, and just burst into laughter. *What the actual fuck were we going to do now?*

The club itself felt like a fever dream. It sat on a golf course and looked like it hadn't been updated since the early 90s, complete with slot machines, Keno screens, and horse betting stations nestled between tables of retirees. The servers floated around in matching bowling shirts, with thick Aussie accents layered over polite indifference. G and I, with our American accents and outfits, looked and felt like complete imposters.

"I can't with this, bro," I whispered, trying to hold it together. "Where the fuck *are* we?"

G cracked up. Just then, our server returned and placed what she called "milkshakes" in front of us.

"Here's these for you gyals," she chirped, flashing a smile.

We looked down.

They weren't milkshakes. They were *ice cream sundaes*—scoops of vanilla stacked into waffle cone bowls, drowning in whipped cream and rainbow sprinkles.

G and I exchanged a look.

"Yummy milkshakes," G said with a straight face, and we both lost it again.

It was all so ridiculous, so perfectly off-script, we couldn't do anything but laugh.

We left the country club still laughing, but knowing we needed to come up with a real plan to salvage the rest of our road trip. Back at our Airbnb, we sat down and checked the forecast one more time. Yep, still nothing but rain up north. So, we pivoted. We'd head back down south, toward clearer skies and sunshine.

That's when Byron Bay came up.

It had been mentioned in passing by nearly every traveler we'd met, and always with a kind of hushed admiration. Locals called it a must see. Fellow backpackers described it as magic. And something about it just stuck.

Byron Bay, like all well-known places, is defined by its people—by the social, economic, and cultural energy they create and carry with them. And if there's anywhere in the world where identities feel like they both collide and coexist in the most beautiful way, it's there.

Byron is equal parts hippie and yuppie. On one side, it is barefoot wanderers meditating on the beach at sunrise, strumming guitars in the park, living out of vans adorned with fairy lights and peace signs. You pass crystal shops on every corner, smell palo Santo drifting from open windows, and see people who look like they've never known a day of rush in their lives. Time feels slower there, like the whole town decided to collectively exhale.

But layered right into that same space are polished, bohemian elites. The yuppies of Byron Bay—wealthy tourists and influencers with designer linen sets and oat milk lattés, shopping in boutiques where "effortless" beachwear somehow costs hundreds of dollars. They're here for the wellness retreats, rooftop cocktails, and sunset yoga. It's spiritual, but curated. Earthy, but expensive.

And somehow, both worlds move side by side, creating a place that feels like it doesn't quite know what it is, and that's exactly what makes it special.

G and I found ourselves existing somewhere in the middle of it all. We spent our days wandering the streets, bouncing between trendy cafés and boutique shops, searching for the perfect dresses to wear for a sunset beach photoshoot. We asked locals for their favorite spots to go out, determined to find a good time even on a Monday night.

The woman at the boutique had suggested a local favorite for live music and drinks: The Northern Hotel. After dinner, G and I wandered into the dimly lit, effortlessly cool bar, the kind of place that didn't need to try too hard. The wooden walls were worn smooth with age, and the air buzzed with an anticipatory energy that hangs in venues right before something special begins.

Scattered around small, round tables were patrons nursing pints of beer and glasses of wine, their silhouettes flickering beneath low-hanging bulbs. In the middle of the room, two older gentlemen, one in a crisp button-down, the other in a faded tee, sat at baby grand pianos facing each other. Their fingers danced across keys with an ease that only comes from a lifetime of playing. Each note felt effortless. They weren't just performing. They were dueling with melodies.

We ordered our usual vodka sodas and scanned the room. A small group sat in the corner booths, but our eyes landed on a table with two guys who were not only singing along but doing so with full commitment.

"Mind if we join you?" I asked, gesturing to the two empty chairs at their table.

"Please!" they said in unison, grinning.

Their names were Tim and Rory—two Aussie carpenters from a rural town outside of Melbourne on a boys' holiday, living out of a camper van and chasing good weather and better nights out. They carried the exact kind of carefree, sun-drenched energy you hope to stumble into in Byron: equal parts laid-back and ready for anything.

Tim, a brunette, had an effortlessly rugged look to him, with kind eyes, and sun-kissed, tattooed skin that told the story of someone who spends most of his life outdoors. His dark hair was styled in a classic Aussie mullet, just messy enough to suggest he hadn't thought twice about it, which somehow made it look even better. He had a magnetic, easygoing charm about him.

And then there was Rory, the golden boy. Blonde hair, casually undone, and a smile that barely left his face all night. His bright blue eyes somehow still caught the glow of the bar's string lights, and he had this subtle, steady warmth about him. He made strangers feel welcome without even trying.

Together, they were the kind of duo that makes an ordinary Monday night feel like something worth remembering.

As we traded stories and pleasantries, I glanced around.

"Wait…why is no one dancing?" I asked. "This place is awesome."

"You're right. Let's fix that," Rory said, already sliding out of his seat.

Tim disappeared to the bar and returned with another round. We scribbled down song suggestions and slipped Australian bills into the jar for the pianists who smoothly transitioned from Elton John to Billy Joel, Queen to Coldplay.

That's when the bar came became alive. Slowly, like a tide rolling in, the rest of the bar began to move. People stood. Strangers clapped. A few more joined the dance floor. And before we knew it, the room had transformed. We weren't just part of the night; we were carrying it.

We waved in people from the street. We clinked glasses with strangers. We belted lyrics like we'd waited our whole lives to sing them. And in that small bar tucked into the heart of Byron Bay, it was as if the world had shrunk to this one room.

At one point, Tim pulled me in close, his hands settling gently at my waist.

"Dance with me?" He asked, though I was already saying yes.

Before I knew it, I was in his arms, swaying under the glow of the warm bar lights. And then, he turned my head towards his and kissed me. The kiss felt magic. Electric. Like a jolt that starts in your toes and shoots all the way through your spine. He held my face in his hands, gently, like he was afraid to break the moment.

While the rest of the bar belted out Rick Springfield and raised their glasses to the night, I was facing Tim lost in a kiss that melted everything else away.

We all have kisses like that. Moments suspended in time that leave a permanent imprint on our hearts, whether we're ready for them or not. It's why fairytales are written. Why rom-coms always have that one scene of the two people who aren't supposed to end up together, running across cities or airports or rain-soaked streets to meet each other in a kiss that makes everything else feel worth it.

Those moments are romanticized, but real. And they matter not because they always lead to forever, but because, in that instant, they remind us of what it means to feel fully alive. To be wanted, seen, held. To lose yourself in something beautiful, even if only for a night.

Eventually, the music inside faded into background music. That kind of magic can't be contained by four walls forever. We were tipsy, glowing, and riding the high of a night that would become one of the best of our lives.

By the time we'd lost track of what number drink we were on, someone, maybe Tim, maybe Rory, suggested we take the party somewhere else. And just like that, we spilled out into the Byron night, laughter trailing behind us.

We walked down to the beach, me hand-in-hand with Tim, G hand-in-hand with Rory. The air was warm with sea-salt, the sand cool beneath our feet.

At the edge of the shore, a pair of girls waved us over to join their bonfire—a loose circle of strangers passing around a guitar and ukulele, singing songs we all half-knew the words to. Someone strummed, someone harmonized, the rest of us leaned back into the sand and simply listened.

There was no actual fire burning, just the remnants of one long extinguished, its embers cold. And yet, the moonlight took over, casting a silver glow across the water and illuminating the faces of strangers who, for reasons I couldn't explain, were unforgettable.

A man from Chile strummed his ukulele, while a French boy free styled in a language most of us didn't understand, his words slightly off-key but no less beautiful. Next to him, a man sat completely naked, tears streaming down his face as he lifted his hands to the sky.

No one flinched. No one turned away. Strangers gathered around him, arms draped over his shoulders, holding him, and embracing him without hesitation and without question.

I don't think anyone knew why he was crying. But the why didn't matter. When a human is that raw—naked, sobbing, surrounded by people he's never met, you don't ask. You just offer presence. You let love become something physical, something you can almost touch in the air around you. Especially in a place like Byron Bay, where people cry without shame, dance without music, and move barefoot beneath the moonlight as if vulnerability is the most natural thing in the world. And maybe it is.

Tim and Rory went from two strangers at a bar to two people I now consider lifelong friends.

By the next morning, the spell of the night hadn't worn off. We sat with our coffees and replayed every detail from the dueling pianos to the barefoot beach walk, the man crying beneath the moonlight, and the way it all felt more like a dream than a memory. We promised to see each other again in Melbourne, even if none of us quite knew what that would look like.

The part that stayed with me most about that night was how the music, the beach, the strangers who became friends, the naked man crying beneath the moonlight all existed without any pretense. It was one of the most human moments of my life. No labels. No résumés. No, "so, what do you do?" It was connection it its rawest form.

Nights like that remind me of how different the world feels when we let people be who they are, instead of what they do. Among travelers, among people who are simply present, the question of,

"What do you do for work?", almost never comes up. It's striking how irrelevant it becomes. People ask where you've been, what you've loved, how the night has felt so far. They ask about stories, not job titles.

It's the opposite of how it often is in the U.S., where the question is practically a reflex—a shortcut to categorizing each other, as if identity begins and ends with a profession. But in Byron Bay, none of that mattered. Not our occupations, or our accomplishments. Not the curated versions of ourselves we carry around in the daylight.

A few days later, G and I wandered into The LUME Melbourne—an immersive museum where the walls came alive with the brushstrokes of Monet and other French Impressionists. Giant projections of water lilies, gardens, and sunlit streets surrounded us, everything soft-edged and glowing, like we'd stepped into someone else's memory.

Impressionist painters didn't try to capture perfect likenesses. They captured feeling. Moments. A woman walking through a garden. A man reading a newspaper. Ordinary people, in ordinary places, rendered in soft strokes: beautiful precisely because they weren't sharp or defined. There was movement in their stillness. Humanity in their blur.

And as I stood there, watching those brushstrokes ripple across the walls, I realized: that's all any of us want, isn't it? To be seen in the in-between. To be known not just for the roles we play, but for the unfinished strokes that make us human. Our thoughts. Our contradictions. The layers beneath us.

None of these things fit neatly into: "So, what do you do for work?"

And funny enough, that realization brought me back to the service industry—the first place I learned how easy it is to miss what's real about a person when you're only looking for a label. Behind every table number, every bar order, every uniform and name tag, there's a life full of color and texture you'll never understand through a job title alone.

Maybe that's why Byron Bay felt so familiar. The people we met lived in that blur too. Tim and Rory weren't "carpenters from outside Melbourne." They were music lovers, dancers, risk-takers, storytellers. They were two men who pulled strangers into laughter. They were brushstrokes, not bullet points.

Just like the Impressionists, they existed in color and movement.

And on that beach, when a naked man cried beneath the moonlight and strangers wrapped their arms around him, no one asked, "So what do you do?" How could they? His pain wasn't a profession. His humanity didn't need a résumé.

The people gathered around that extinguished bonfire were like a living painting—imperfect, luminous, blending into one another.

Because who someone is has never been contained in their job or the quick summary they offer when first asked. We're made of subtler things in the way we laugh, the way we reach for others, the way we soften or glow in certain kinds of light. Those are the details that tell the truth.

And yet for years, I introduced myself through labels: *Hi, I'm Bella. I'm a daughter, a sister, a writer, a traveler, a friend.* They mattered—they gave shape to my story—but they were still shortcuts, ways of making myself legible to someone else. What I know now is that who we are lives beneath all of that. In the in-between. In the contradictions. In the parts that refuse a neat introduction. The truth isn't in the labels we wear, but in what spills beyond their edges.

That's the version of people I want to meet more often. The one untouched by expectations, roles, or titles. The one simply being human. And that's what G understood. She didn't wait for extraordinary moments to see people. She did it in the ordinary ones—in the middle of dinner rushes, under harsh restaurant lighting, receipts stacked in her apron. She made humanness the point.

Maybe that's the work of a lifetime: loosening our grip on the definitions we wear so comfortably. Letting them breathe. Honoring what they offer without letting them eclipse who we're becoming. Seeing labels for what they are—doorways, not destinations. If we're lucky, we grow out of some, choose new ones, and become versions of ourselves we never expected. The ones that don't show up on paper, but reveal themselves in how we love, how we show up, how we see.

Because we are all evolving, all the time. And the most honest thing we can do is stay open. Let ourselves surprise us.

Who am I becoming? Who have I been? And who might I still be, if I let myself?

Chapter 5: Child's Play

Dear Reader,

When we were young, we knew how to play. We ran barefoot through our backyards, built kingdoms out of cushions, and turned bathwater into oceans. We didn't question if we were too loud, too messy, too much. We danced when music played and cried when we were hurt, without shame or explanation. We were, in every way, fully ourselves—curious, honest, soft, brave.

The younger version of ourselves lives within all of us. You can hear it in music, feel it in poetry, catch glimpses of it in films—this ache to be 'forever young', just like Alphaville sings. It's more than nostalgia. It's remembering. A reaching—to return to the part of us that once believed life was magic and love was simple.

This chapter is a love letter to that child. To the wildness we try to discipline. To the ache that still longs to be chosen. To the joy that once needed no permission. It's also about how, as adults, our most erotic and emotional longings are often rooted in the same hunger: to be fully known, fully felt, fully free.

Because healing doesn't always look like meditating on a mountaintop or rewriting your childhood narrative. Sometimes, healing is laughter in the silliest things. It's letting someone touch a part of you you'd been hiding—not just your body, but your spirit.

This chapter is about finding our way back to play, not just the kind with toys and games, but the kind where love is unguarded, presence is pure, and the world feels safe enough to let your guard down.

✳✳✳

Sex is one of the most primal, human acts there is, and yet, for something so universal, so foundational to our very existence, we rarely talk about it in all its complexity. We joke about it. We fear it. We obsess over it. But we don't often sit with it. With the messiness of it, the vulnerability, the sheer animal truth that it is the reason we are all here.

And for something so instinctive, it's remarkable how deeply personal, and varied, our relationships to sex can be. Few parts of our lives carry as much tension between instinct and identity, biology and belief.

Sexuality touches nearly every part of who we are. Not just in the physical sense, but in how we see ourselves, how we relate to others, how we express intimacy, power, vulnerability, and desire. It's not just about biology, or acts of sex, or reproduction. It's about the complicated ways our wants take shape. About the beliefs we carry, inherited or learned, around pleasure, shame, connection, and worth.

Our sexuality isn't something separate from who we are. It's woven into our personalities, our relationships, our fears, our fantasies. The way we love, the way we touch, the way we long, it all mirrors our values, our wounds, and our truths. To understand our sexuality, then, is to understand something much deeper than sex. It's to understand ourselves.

I was walking through the Kunsthistoriches Museum in Vienna, Austria when I came across Daniel Munich's marble sculpture titled: "Cupids Playing". The sculpture depicts three winged children, locked in play, their innocence frozen in stone. At first glance, it felt harmless, pure. The kind of image meant to remind us of the lightness of childhood. But there was something else there, too. A tension between their smiles. A flicker in their eyes that didn't feel entirely innocent.

And then I saw the inscription beneath them, suggesting that their play was more than just a game—it was a mirror. A reflection of adult desires: erotic, complicated, consuming. A foreshadowing of the passions and longings we carry with us into adulthood.

I thought about how often our earliest templates for intimacy are laid in childhood. Not in a sexual way, but in the way we learn to be seen, to be touched, to be wanted. The way we play. The way we form bonds. The way we ache to be chosen. We don't talk enough about how those early needs evolve into the longings we later feel as adults.

What if sex, at its most human level, isn't just about pleasure, but about remembering how to play? About returning to the wild and unfiltered parts of ourselves that existed before shame and performance crept in.

I met my best friend Clancy when we were just fourteen, the summer before starting high school. It was our first dance team practice and we'd both just made the junior varsity squad.

She introduces herself to most people with the same wide, infectious smile: "Hi! I'm Clancy!"

There's almost always a pause. A flicker of confusion.

"Clancy?" They'll ask, tilting their head to make sure they heard that right.

And without missing a beat, she'll chime back, "Yes! Clancy—like Nancy, but with a C!"

Clancy, in Gaelic, means "red-headed warrior," and there could not be a more fitting name. She was (and still is) all sunshine. She is bubbly, bright, bursting with color. A firecracker in a five-foot-four frame, with a crown of beautiful red curls that bounce with every step she takes.

From our very first practice, we became inseparable. Our friendship moved fast, the way all the best ones do at fourteen. We grew up together over those four years, orbiting each other like two planets that somehow shared the same sun. We talked about everything from crushes to the latest dance team drama, and all the lives we imagined for ourselves beyond the hallways, homecomings, and pep rallies.

We attended an all-girls Catholic school called Regis Jesuit, where polos and khakis were our daily uniform and gossip spread faster than morning announcements. The boys' division sat just across campus, close enough to wave at across the courtyard, but far enough to feel like another universe. And even though we spent most of our days separated by brick walls and theology class, we still always found ways to drift toward that universe.

After school, before dance practice, we'd usually find a reason to wander into the boys' building, always out of our polos and into our little shorts and dance tanks. There was something thrilling about those moments: the quick glances in the hallways, the echo of laughter that wasn't supposed to be heard, the awareness of wanting to be noticed.

It's kind of ironic how, in a place designed to keep us apart, we always found ways to slip through the cracks. We learned early that attraction could be both playful and powerful, that curiosity itself felt exhilarating.

At the same time, being separated from the boys created a kind of freedom we didn't recognize then but I'm grateful for now. In that environment, we could focus on our education, our friendships, and ourselves. We could raise our hands and ask questions without worrying about looking silly in front of a crush. We could show up to school with messy hair, no makeup, and the confidence of knowing that how we looked didn't define us that day. There was a power in that. It was a space to exist fully as ourselves without the constant performance of girlhood.

Regis was a place that challenged us, shaped us, and sent us into the world believing we could change it. Its Jesuit motto: "Go forth and set the world on fire", felt dramatic at the time, but it stuck. It was a place that gave us the permission and purpose to be curious, to be brave, and to burn brightly when the time came.

However, as prepared as we thought we were, we still lived inside a kind of blissful ignorance—one that kept the realities of the world just outside those campus walls. Life was simple and joyful.

But it was also safe and predictable. Life's messier lessons were still waiting for us, far beyond the courtyard.

Looking back, I think that was where it began. Our first, clumsy brush with sexuality. We didn't have words for it then, but sneaking over to the boys' school, laughing too loudly, caring how we looked, those were all early rehearsals in wanting. In play. And in learning how to be seen.

Clancy and I stayed close throughout college, always finding our way back to each other during school breaks, long phone calls, and spontaneous visits. We swapped stories of late nights, heartbreaks, bad decisions, and brilliant ones. Our bond never wavered.

College came with its own set of challenges with new freedoms, new expectations, and an unspoken pressure to have it all figured out. At first, it felt exciting. But as the novelty of frat party basements, naps at 1 p.m., and no Friday classes wore off, the edges of reality began to show. Adulthood came with a lot of uncertainty.

By the time we reached our twenties, that uncertainty had become its own language. Clancy and I, like most of our friends, were learning that life after graduation wasn't all sunshine and rainbows. The same girls who once ruled the hallways, were now silently wondering if they'd chosen the right major, the right city, the right life. It wasn't just about jobs or futures, it was about who we were becoming, what we wanted, and how to find meaning in a world that suddenly felt so wide and undefined.

One of our friends, Caitlyn, once called it the "twenties struggle boat"—a perfect image for what it felt like to be floating in open water, unsure which direction to row or whether you even want to be on the boat you're in at all. She said it one night while buried in job applications, half-laughing through the frustration of feeling stuck. We all laughed too but it stuck with me. We were all just trying to captain our own versions of that same leaky boat.

And when college flew by even faster than high school did, the world didn't open up in the limitless ways we'd been promised. Everyone had an opinion: Apply now. Take time off. Find stability. Take risks while you're young. Settle down. Explore. Choose wisely, but don't wait too long. Every decision suddenly felt like a fork in the road we hadn't studied for, and the stakes seemed impossibly high.

"I'm just really trying to receive what the universe is teaching me," Clancy texted me one night while she was living and teaching in New York City. "I'm trying to figure out how to heal myself, but it's really hard and not what I expected of my life, or my 20s."

Two years after graduating college, Clancy had moved to New York to work as a teaching fellow at an inner-city school for girls. It was supposed to be a bold new chapter, a leap toward purpose and passion. But almost as soon as she arrived, her body began to rebel. A string of unresolved health issues surfaced, forcing her to scale back and, eventually move back home to Denver. With the physical symptoms came waves of anxiety, questions that spiraled heavier each day: *Am I even meant to do this? Am I strong enough for this work? Did I make a mistake?*

It's always fascinated me how intricately our bodies, minds, and souls are wired together. When we're out of alignment, when we're living in places or relationships or roles that no longer serve us, our bodies don't stay silent. They speak to us in symptoms. They scream through illness. They ask us to pay attention in ways we can't ignore.

For Clancy, that dissonance between her internal world and external environment became impossible to overlook. Her anxiety didn't just linger in her head, it settled into her body. It made it hard to breathe, hard to sleep, hard to function. Eventually, it pulled her home.

It reminded me of something I had almost forgotten. A moment from high school our senior year just after third period. The hallways were their usual cacophony of chaos: locker doors slamming, sneakers squeaking across linoleum floors, half-eaten granola bars shoved into backpacks. Girls shuffled past in every direction, their laughter bouncing off the walls. Through the crowd, I saw Clancy. Her face was red and blotchy, her curly hair frizzed around her. She moved toward me panicked, her whole body trembling, her breaths coming in short, frantic gasps.

Without a word, I grabbed her hand and gently guided her away from the chaos, ducking us into the nearest open classroom. The door clicked shut behind us, muffling the hallway noise. The room was empty, dimly lit by the weak daylight filtering through closed blinds. Clancy stood in front of me, gasping for air like she was trapped inside her own body.

I placed a steady hand on her back. "Hey. Look at me, Clanc," I said softly. "Just breathe. You're okay. Breathe with me."

I slowed my own breathing deliberately, exaggerating the rise and fall of my chest so she could match it. Inhale, hold, exhale. Over and over. I kept my eyes on hers. Eventually, the color began to return to her face. Her breath steadied.

We stood there in silence for a few minutes, the hum of fluorescent lights filling the quiet. I didn't ask what had triggered it, I knew she'd tell me when she was ready. In that moment, she didn't need answers. She just needed safety.

Years later, I asked Clancy if she remembered that moment. To me, it had become etched into memory, a sacred snapshot of our friendship. It felt so tender, so human. Clancy didn't remember. But that was okay.

Because what mattered wasn't the details. It was the pattern. The way her body spoke when words couldn't. The way fear lodged itself in her chest and asked to be seen. And all these years later, it was happening again, just in a different setting, with higher stakes.

The classroom had become a crowded subway car. The linoleum floors replaced by Manhattan pavement. Instead of whispering "just breathe" between class bells, we were texting across times zones, trying to hold space for each other from afar.

And still, it was the same Clancy. The uncertainty of your twenties isn't just uncomfortable, it's disorienting. No one warns you that the real growing begins *after* the cap and gown. That there's no syllabus for self-worth. No midterm for clarity. Just a vague map scribbled with shoulds and maybes and deadlines that don't actually exist.

It's a decade defined by decision fatigue, identity shifts, and the unspoken grief of outgrowing old versions of ourselves before we've figured out what the new one looks like. Clancy was in the thick of the "twenties struggle boat". And I knew that boat, too.

We all did.

At the time, I was studying in London and living across an ocean made it hard to comfort her the way I wanted to. Like so many of my friends and family, she was struggling in her own way, and all I could offer were late-night texts, voice notes, or a shaky FaceTime call. Still, it was a reminder that distance didn't mean absence.

Sometimes those reminders came as old photos and videos, shared like tiny lifelines to simpler times. "Remember this?" we'd write. It was more than nostalgia; it was a way of reaching back toward the parts of ourselves that once felt whole. A kind of love letter to our inner child.

As I've grown older, I've come to understand that healing that child doesn't always look like therapy or meditation. Sometimes it's laughter that spills out unexpectedly, or dancing to the songs you once blasted in your bedroom, or calling the friend who knew you before the world told you who to be.

When Clancy moved back home after leaving New York, she started seeking out spaces that helped her reconnect with that version of herself. The playful, curious, unguarded one. By the time I returned to Denver from London later that summer, I met a new Clancy who was softer in some ways, and stronger in others.

She was working at a crystal shop, surrounded by shelves of gemstones, incense, and intention-setting candles. It was the kind of place people wandered into when they were searching for healing, for clarity, for connection. Her coworkers, who were mostly queer, carried energies that reflected the shop itself— warm, grounding, and a little mystical.

Working at the shop gave Clancy the space to step into something she'd never explored before. Surrounded by people who honored fluidity and intuition, she began to question what she had always assumed about herself. Slowly, she opened to the idea of loving people of different sexual and gender identities beyond the narrow, heteronormative framework we'd both been taught to attach to.

As her best friend, it was a beautiful thing to witness. After months of hearing only pain and confusion through phone calls and voice memos, I finally walked into that crystal shop and saw a version of Clancy that felt both brand new and deeply familiar. It was like catching a glimpse of the fourteen-year-old I'd first met in our high school gym, only now she was brighter, fuller, and more herself.

Watching her, I realized how cyclical it all was—the curiosity, the play, the longing to be seen. What started in those hallways at Regis had grown into something braver and more expansive: the freedom to explore desire without shame, and to rediscover the joy that comes from simply being alive in your own body.

I watched her float around the shop, introducing me to the people who now formed her chosen community. She moved with a confidence I hadn't seen in years. At one point, she pulled me aside, a mischievous grin spreading across her face.

"I have the biggest crush on someone named Ryann," she whispered. "They're non-binary…and I've never felt so much sexual tension in my life."

That was how Clancy came out to me. Not in a big, dramatic sit-down, but in a way a fourteen-year-old might confess their first crush.

A few months later, she and Ryann began dating. It was her first queer relationship, and in many ways, her first real relationship. Ryann was healing for Clancy in more ways than one. They didn't just love her for who she already was; they made space for who she was becoming. It was a relationship where she was able to exist freely.

Of all the sweet things Clancy shared about their relationship— the comfort, the chemistry, the laughter—what she emphasized most was how healing it felt for her inner child.

"It's just… so much play, all the time," she told me one day, her voice lit up like sunshine. "Ryann built me this miniature fairy dollhouse for my birthday. Look how it shines."

We were sitting cross-legged on her couch coloring when she turned her phone toward me to show a photo: tiny glittering walls, soft moss, fairy-sized trinkets tucked into corners. It looked like something out of a dream, a forgotten corner of childhood come back to life.

In that moment, I realized their love wasn't just about romance, it was about reclamation. It was about Clancy returning to the parts of herself that had dimmed over the years and letting them laugh again. Create again. Trust again.

Watching her step into this new version of herself brought so much to light. There was joy in her again. The way she moved through her first queer relationship reminded me of something so simple, so vital: play. Not just laughter or silliness, though there was plenty of that, but a deeper kind of play—the kind born of safety, curiosity, and the rare gift of being fully seen and still chosen.

And that brought me right back to those afternoons at Regis when Clancy and I would sneak across campus, laughing too loud, hearts racing at the sight of the boys' school doors. We thought we were chasing attention, but really, we were beginning to explore the edges of who we might become.

That's what the *Cupids Playing* sculpture in Vienna had been suggesting all along. The way the angels' innocence held a shadow of something more, was a foreshadowing of all the longing and tenderness that will always live inside us. Innocence and desire, not in conflict, but in harmony.

Because whether we're queer, straight, questioning, partnered, or alone, intimacy in its most honest form is a return to the rawest and most tender parts of us—the parts that still remember what it means to play. Maybe sex, love, connection, all of it, is just a grown-up version of child's play. Curious. Full of wonder. Willing to be messy, and awkward, and new.

Part Two: Letters from the World

Chapter 6: When the World Says Hello

Dear Reader,

There's something powerful about moving through the world on your own. When you travel solo, you carry your life in a backpack—your thoughts, your emotions, your stories—and you learn to listen, not just to your surroundings, but to yourself. You notice what your body needs, what your heart longs for, and what your soul has been whispering all along.

But maybe the most surprising part of being alone is how often you're not. How the world has a way of showing up for you. A stranger offers direction and ends up sharing their life story. You sit next to someone in your hostel's kitchen and somehow conversation flows like you've known them forever. You laugh with someone whose language you don't speak but you understand each other perfectly.

This chapter is about those moments. The serendipitous ones that remind us we are never as isolated as we think. It's about the unexpected friends, the shared meals with strangers, and the unplanned adventures that no itinerary could have prepared you for. It's about listening to your gut when it tells you to stay a little longer, to take a different street, or to just say yes.

It's also about knowing when to rest. When to honor the heaviness in your chest. When your body begs for stillness, and your heart needs solitude more than stimulation.

So, as you read this chapter, I invite you to think back on the people and moments that changed you, no matter how brief. The ones that reminded you the world isn't so big, or so lonely, after all. And if you're still waiting for that moment, trust that it's coming. Sometimes, all it takes is one step, one smile, one yes… and suddenly the world says hello.

The question is: will you be open enough to say hello back?

***

After nearly a year of living in London, I had spent plenty of time learning how to be alone without feeling lonely. I had built a life. One filled with chosen routines, friendships, and resilience I didn't know I had. London had become my anchor, a place that had both tested and transformed me. I was no longer the wide-eyed girl who first arrived, unsure and overwhelmed. I had grown steadier, softer, and more curious.

So, when I set off on a three-week trip through the south of France and northern Italy, I figured I knew what solitude looked like—I'd lived it. But solo travel is a different kind of alone. There's no home to return to at night. No familiar coffee shops. No group chat itching with plans. Just you, a backpack, and the unsettling freedom of not knowing exactly what comes next.

But at first, I wasn't alone. This was the same trip that Olly and I had planned together. We had our trains booked, routes mapped, and accommodation secured. But even the best-laid plans unravel.

Before everything fell apart, though, there was Montpellier.

It was our first stop where we weren't in our own little bubble. Up until that point, Olly and I had stayed in private Airbnb's, just the two of us. But in Montpellier, we checked into a hostel and the shift was instant. The energy was lighter. We were surrounded by other travelers, and for the first time on our journey, we were finally part of something bigger than just the two of us.

I remember lying in my bunk, both my phone and social battery plugged in, half-tuned out but still listening. Olly had just come out of the communal shower and started chatting with two guys in the room.

"Ah yep, we've just started our trip—traveling for about a month or so we are," said one of the boys, his Northern Irish accent thick.

"Yeah sweet," Olly replied. "We've only just arrived in Montpellier to stop for the night. Started in Marseille, hired a car. We've been driving all over. Just spent the day walking around Aix-en-Provence."

Classic hostel chat: Where are you from? Where are you headed? How long are you on the road? It was comforting in its predictability, the same script repeated all over the world in dorm rooms filled with half-zipped backpacks and clothes draped over railings to dry.

I stayed quiet at first, scrolling through my camera roll and casually composing my next Instagram post, waiting for the right moment to jump in.

"We're headed to Nice in a few days," said the other Northern Irish boy. "Then to Genova, Rome, and some of the southern bits of Italy too."

At the mention of Rome, I poked my head out from behind the bunk curtain, eyes lighting up, and looked over at Olly.

"We met in Rome," we both said at the same time, motioning toward each other with a grin.

"Do you know where you're staying at yet?" I added.

One of the boys pulled out his phone, scrolling for a second before turning it toward Olly. "Uh…this one."

Olly looked down, then glanced up at me with a soft, knowing smile. He turned back to the guys, laughing slightly.

"Yeah. That's the hostel we stayed at over two years ago now. That's mad."

The four of us exchanged Instagrams and spent the rest of the evening in a bar nearby, drinking pints of Guinness and watching the opening night of the EuroCup. Cole and Luke, the two Irish boys, took it upon themselves to educate us on the sacred art of European football—who to root for, who not to, and why the tournament was practically a national holiday back home.

The next morning, Olly and I left early. We didn't make any promises to meet up again. The boys had casually mentioned they'd be heading to Nice around the same time we were. At the time, it felt like one of those fun, fleeting hostel coincidences. Nothing more.

But just a few days later, I would remember that moment differently.

Because just forty-eight hours after Montpellier, everything fell apart in Cannes.

The dramas of leaving Olly in Cannes were exhausting and consuming. I had tried, really tried, to hold myself together. But when the dynamic turned heavy and unsteady, I knew it was time to walk away. To choose myself. To protect my peace, even if it broke my heart a little.

The adrenaline of it all—the tension, the unraveling, and then leaving, left me scattered. My body was anxious as ever, my mind racing but blank. I couldn't even begin to think about what came next.

It was around 3 p.m. in Cannes when I found myself alone in a small bar. It was just me and four older French men silently watching the world go by. I had stopped in for a beer, some Wi-Fi, and a moment to breathe. Everyone I was close to in London was wrapped up in their own day, and most of my friends and family back in Denver were still asleep. I needed someone to talk to.

So, I FaceTimed my grandma, who was just an hour ahead staying with my aunt in Minnesota.

She answered on the second ring, already talking to my aunt Christine. "Oh, Bella's calling me!" She said excitedly, her face filling the screen, not realizing she'd already accepted the call.

"Hi, Bell! Where are you?"

"I'm in Cannes right now, Grandma, but… everything just went to shit."

I told her the whole story—what had happened with Olly, how it all unraveled so fast in the last few hours, how I suddenly had nowhere to go.

"Oh my god, Bella. I can't believe that" she said, her voice rising with a protecting urgency. "I'm so sorry. What are you going to do?"

"I don't know. Pretty much everything we booked is under his name. I might just fly back to London. I don't know what else to do."

"Oh, you can't do that," she said firmly, and right on cue, my aunt leaned into the frame.

"You can't let him ruin your trip," she added. "How much longer were you supposed to be traveling for?"

"Another two weeks. I don't want to go back to London, but I'm also so unsure of what to do next."

My grandma is not your typical, cookie-baking, sweater-making, grandma. Ever since my grandpa passed away ten years ago, my grandma has travelled solo. She spends half the year in her condo in Mazatlán, Mexico—playing tennis in the morning, sipping margaritas in the late-afternoon sun, and making friends with anyone half as outgoing as she is. She has friends scattered around the world and is always invited to weddings, baby showers, and neighborhood luncheons. For all her worldliness, she remains a fiercely loyal friend and the best grandmother I could ask for—rooted in connection even as she chases the horizon.

She can't sit still if her life depended on it. If she stays in one place too long, you can practically feel her energy bursting with restlessness. Her next adventure is always booked months in advance—flights highlighted on her calendar, notes scribbled on papers all throughout her kitchen counter, suitcases packed in every room of her house. Her main residence is Denver, but she even treats coming home like an expedition. She reports back on her time away with the same excitement most people reserve for safaris (which she's been on many by the way), and if you want to see her, you'd better ask where you can wedge yourself into her already full social itinerary.

My grandma has passed down many genes to me, but my favorite one will always be her travel bug. At 81 years old, she is not slowing down. In fact, she seems to be picking up speed, as if she's racing time itself and somehow winning.

So, despite the generational gap between us, I knew she would understand all the feelings I was grappling with. And she did.

Together, she and my aunt booked me a hotel in Nice. Two nights. Just enough to rest, reset, and figure out what I needed to do next.

I walked into the hotel with my 12kg backpack that had been strapped to me all day. My back ached. My feet throbbed. I was exhausted in every possible way: mentally, emotionally, physically.

When I finally stepped into the room, I let it all go. I dropped the bag, collapsed onto the queen-sized bed, and just lay there, staring at the ceiling. The quiet felt almost suspicious. I took a few long, steady breaths, letting the stillness settle into my chest.

Eventually, I called my parents to give them an update on the hell of a day I'd just survived. I filled them in on everything—some parts rushed; others still too raw to say out loud.

Then I showered. Let the hot water wash off the sweat, the stress, the confusion. I stepped out feeling a little more like myself.

And that's when I remembered: Cole and Luke.

The two Northern Irish boys had just arrived in Nice as well, so I messaged them. I filled them in on the whole situation with Olly and told them I'd made the decision to keep traveling on my own. Their response was immediate and warm. They were proud of me for sticking it out and invited me to meet up for more Guinness and European football.

Their Irish spirit was exactly what I needed.

What had started as one of the worst days of my trip slowly transformed into one of the best nights. We danced on top of tables to live music until three in the morning, the rhythm shaking something loose in me. The stress, the heaviness, and the heartbreak had all melted into laughter, movement, and music.

In that moment, I felt the magic return. The part of me that loved adventure, loved connection, loved being fully in a moment, I remembered who I was before the drama—before I started doubting my place in the story.

Cole and Luke became constants throughout the rest of my trip. They didn't just know the details of what had happened, they understood the emotional aftermath. They knew when to ask questions and when to just hand me a drink, because anything could be fixed with a pint of Guinness. They didn't let me spiral or stay stuck in discouraging thoughts.

They were my first sign from the universe that I wasn't alone.

And from that moment on, I had officially begun to settle into my very first solo adventure.

After my two nights in Nice, my only plan was a one-night stay at a hostel in Genova, Italy.

Genova is a city made of narrow, winding streets—a beautiful maze that isn't necessarily polished or postcard-perfect, but it's real. Lived in. The kind of place where the past feels just barely tucked beneath the surface. The alleyways are lined with crumbling pastel buildings, their windows draped with laundry fluttering in the breeze like flags.

My hostel was tucked away in one of these alleyways, inside a 14th-century building on a path that, at first, seemed a little sketchy. I climbed up a steep, shadowy lane, half-convinced I was going the wrong way until I spotted the first small sign. It pointed me up the stairs. Then another. And another.

I kept climbing the winding staircases that twisted through the old building. After each flight, I thought maybe I'd made it. Nope. One more. And then another. By the fourth flight, sweating and out of breath, I finally reached the top.

Federico and Mateo, the Italian brothers who owned the hostel, greeted me at the front desk.

"Hi, I'm checking in," I said, still trying to catch my breath, "The name is Bella Scipione."

"*Ship-ee-own-ay!!*" They shouted in unison, rolling the name off their tongues the proper Italian way.

"*Sei italiana, no?*" Mateo asked, his eyes lighting up.

I smiled. "Well…" I replied in English, "my ancestors are from Roma, but no—I'm American."

"Ahh, okay! But do you speak Italian then?"

I blushed, slightly embarrassed. "I know *grazie* and *prego?*"

They both laughed. "Hahaha! Well, Bella. *Benvenuta* to Genoa. We're happy to have you."

Mateo glanced at the computer screen. "But I see you're only staying one night?"

"Yeah," I said with a shrug. "Honestly, I didn't know what to expect from Genova. I have no real plan."

"*No piano?!*" Federico clutched his heart dramatically. "You must stay at least two nights. We have room here. There's too much to see. We'll show you around."

I obliged.

The hostel was unlike any I'd stayed in before. It felt more like a shared house, with just four rooms, a communal kitchen, and a cozy living space where everyone naturally gravitated. After I'd settled in and taken a much-needed power nap, I joined the rest of the hostel for drinks.

Around twelve solo travelers from all over the world were gathered at a long table—sharing stories, comparing itineraries.

Maybe it was because I'd grown so used to traveling with G, or maybe it was something about the atmosphere of Genova and the warmth of that hostel, but for the first time, I truly noticed just how many people were out in the world traveling on their own. And not just surviving but thriving. There was a curious confidence about it. A kind of freedom that wasn't loud or showy, but deeply rooted in self-trust.

Genova is a unique city. It's gritty and graceful, layered with history and life. Once a dominant maritime republic, it played a leading role in commercial trade between the 12th and 15th centuries. A true Mediterranean crossroads, Genova has always been a meeting place—for goods, for people, for cultures. And you can feel it, even now.

The city's spirit of unity runs deep. In fact, during World War II, after five years of suffering under Nazi occupation, Genova become the only Italian city where an entire German army corps surrendered directly to the partisans of the Resistance. That legacy of strength, solidarity, and community still pulses through the city's alleyways and piazzas.

Family and connection remain at the heart of Genovese life, and it shows. You feel it in the way strangers talk to each other, in the way a simple dinner becomes a shared experience. In the way people instinctively make space for one another.

And that's what made Genova so powerful for me. In a moment when I had every reason to feel untethered, the city offered me a sense of belonging. It wrapped around me with its history, its people, and its energy and reminded me that even in solo travel, we don't exist in isolation.

That night, surrounded by a dozen solo travelers, each of us from different countries, speaking different languages, carrying different reasons for being there, I felt a new perspective begin to surface. I wasn't just getting through the trip anymore; I was finally in it. I was learning to be alone without being lonely. To enjoy the quiet as much as the conversation.

Mateo had taken us all to the SUQ Festival—a weekly celebration in June that filled Genova's waterfront with food stalls, music, and cultural performances honoring intercultural dialogue and fundamental human rights. The energy was magnetic. I bounced between conversations with my hostel mates, danced with strangers under strings of festival lights, and then, quietly took a moment to slip away.

I wandered toward the dock, drawn by the hush of the water. The music faded behind me, replaced by the soft hum of the harbor. Boats bobbed in the distance. The sky was painted in the deep blues and golds of a city exhaling after a long day. I stood alone, the cool stone beneath my feet, and let my body be still. My thoughts caught up to me.

I thought about everything that had brought me here: the chaos of Cannes, the leap of continuing the trip alone, the tiny moments—like this one—that were starting to stitch together something meaningful.

Solo traveling had begun to bring out my introverted side, the part of me that tends to surface when I feel overwhelmed and overstimulated. Navigating unfamiliar cities, making decisions alone, and staying open to connection while also tending to my own needs was more tiring that I'd expected.

A lot of people are surprised to learn I'm fundamentally introverted. I love meaningful conversations and thrive in social settings, but solitude has always been a part of me. Since I was a little girl, I've found peace in my own company. And now, on the road, I was learning to honor that side of myself like never before.

In many ways, solo travel became a way of caring for my inner child—nurturing the quieter parts of me, the parts that didn't always get attention in the noise of everyday life. I started to recognize when I needed to recharge, when I needed to be still, when I simply needed to listen instead of speak.

After Genova, I began to move differently, more in tune, more grounded. Still solo, but now with a steadier flow. My steps weren't quite so hesitant. The stillness no longer felt sharp or hollow.

I finished out the final two weeks of my trip exploring Milan, Venice, Madrid, Barcelona, and Palma de Mallorca—meeting friends I'll remember forever, missing trains that forced me to slow down and breathe and figuring out what to do next in the in-between moments. I hiked through the backwoods of Mallorca with three girls I'd met the night before, sneaking into a fancy Hilton hotel like we were cast in some sort of indie coming-of-age film. I'd get caught up in a crush with a cute German boy, both of us fantasizing about what life would look like if we had lived in the same city.

All the while, I was developing a new kind of self-awareness, a gentle kind. One that doesn't announce itself loudly but shows up in the way I move through the world now. With softness. With intention. With a sense of trust in myself.

Drawing from past experiences—from the girl I used to be and the woman I'm still becoming—I've started to shape a version of myself I truly admire. Solo travel didn't just show me the world. It showed me, *me*.

And maybe that's what this whole journey has been about.

Learning to trust my own rhythm. To say no when something doesn't feel right. To say yes when my gut tells me go. To let go of control, to let in wonder. To be okay with not knowing exactly where I'm headed next, and to believe that I'll be okay when I get there.

So, wherever you are—on a train, in a crowded café, or sitting quietly with yourself—I hope you remember this: the world has a way of showing up for you when you start showing up for yourself.

I hope you give yourself permission to do the same. To be bold enough to sit in the discomfort. To trust yourself enough to wander off plan. To listen to your body when it says rest. To listen to your heart when it says stay. To let the world meet you in ways you never expected.

Because when you say yes to being on your own, you start to see everything differently. Including yourself.

So, go.

Book the ticket.

Pack light.

Leave space for the unknown.

And when the world says hello, be brave enough to say hello back.

Chapter 7: Postcards from People I Miss

Dear Reader,

There's a certain kind of ache that comes from loving people who don't live in your city anymore, or maybe never did to begin with. It's a nostalgic kind. The kind that shows up when you hear a song you once sang in the back of an Uber together, or when a sunset feels too beautiful not to share, and you instinctively reach for your phone to send a picture across time zones.

I never realized how many versions of myself I would leave behind in the places I've been, or how many pieces of my heart would live in other people. Friends who feel like home, even from across oceans. People I've shared cheap wine, beds, and secrets with. People I don't see every day, some that have made me laugh so hard until I cry.

This chapter is for the friendships that stretch across maps. For the group chats that never sleep. For the tearful airport hugs, the missed birthdays, the late-night voice memos, the carefully crafted "thinking of you" texts. For the kind of love that doesn't fade with distance but grows through it.

Because sometimes, the people who knew us then are the ones who hold us together now. And maybe home isn't always a place, it's a collection of people scattered across cities and time zones whose laughs you can still hear when something ridiculous happens, even if they're half a world away.

✳✳✳

It was a warm October Saturday night in London. The rain sprinkled, the streets glistened, and the air felt like it was holding on to summer for just a little bit longer.

I was alone in my 30-by-50-foot room, curled up in bed, watching *Gossip Girl* for what was probably the fifth time through. My phone vibrated lazily beside me. It was 10 p.m. I hadn't made plans, but I remembered something my friend Molly had mentioned the night before.

"There's this gay club called Heaven," she'd said. "A few of my friends are going tomorrow night. You should come."

103

It had been one of those vague, friendly kind of mentions where you're not sure if it was an actual invitation or just something said in passing. And now, sitting there in nothing but my oversized hoodie and an oddly specific homesick feeling, I wasn't sure if I'd be crashing the night or just showing up uninvited.

That's when my mom called.

"Hey, Bell! What're you up to tonight?"

"Oh, not much," I replied. "My friend Molly mentioned she and her friends were going to this club, but I don't know if I'm actually invited. I feel weird inviting myself."

"What time is it over there?"

I glanced at the clock and laughed. "Ten."

"Oh please, that's early. You should definitely go. Why not?"

And honestly, she was right. Moms always are.

Why not? I loved dancing. I loved a good club night. And if I was going to feel lonely, I might as well feel lonely somewhere with a good DJ and flashing lights.

I hung up, threw on some pants, and marched myself down the three flights of stairs to the bodega next to my building.

"One 75 ml Bacardi, please. And this," I added, pointing to a chilled can of lemon San Pellegrino.

I walked back to my shoebox of a room with purpose and a pre-party buzz already starting to build in my chest. I slipped into my lucky black skort and white bodysuit, swiped on some makeup, and added a few pieces of jewelry. Nothing too fancy, just enough to feel like I'd made an effort.

My speaker was blasting Lady Gaga and Rihanna, filling the room with just the right vibe to get me in the mood. I poured myself a couple of shots of Bacardi, chasing them with sips of sparkling lemon. Admittedly, I'd done this enough times to have my solo pregame routine pretty dialed in.

By 11:33 p.m., I was out the door, bag in hand. On my way down the stairs, I snapped a quick mirror selfie and sent it to my mom with a caption that said, *Here I go, wish me luck.*

I strutted the eight-minute walk to the tube station, confident with liquid courage pumping through my veins. I found a seat on the Central line of the tube, my headphones in still playing tunes to keep my energy up. When I arrived at my stop 25 minutes later, I had no idea where I was going or what to look for. Thank God for Apple Maps and a random Italian guy who pointed me in the right direction.

I showed up just after midnight and was shocked at the line that was still wrapped around the block. Girls, gays, and theys were dressed to the nines, every outfit a perfect snapshot of personality and self-expression. Sequins, mesh, leather, glitter. And here I was, solo, already tipsy, standing on the outside of something that felt electric.

I respected the line. I really did. But there was no way I—one single, sexy, semi-bold girl—was going to wait. I started at the back and slowly worked my way forward, cutting here and there, mostly unnoticed. Most people were far too drunk or distracted to care. Within five minutes, I was inside.

At the top of the stairs, I stopped, stunned. And somehow, by some miracle or pure dumb luck, I spotted Molly almost instantly through the blur of flashing lights and pulsing bass.

Her whole face lit up when she saw me. She waved me over, shouting, "I cannot believe I found you so soon! I'm so glad you made it!" Her mixed Australian-South African-British accent cut through the music just enough. Molly and I had connected in a Facebook group before I moved to London; we met during my first week and became fast friends. Born in South Africa, raised in Australia, finished high school in the Netherlands—she was an international legend with a worldview I admired.

"Thanks for letting me join! This place is insane!" I yelled as we hugged.

"Right?! Come on, let's dance!" She grabbed my had and headed toward the stage.

Before I knew it, I was on the stage with my sunglasses on, the bass hitting perfectly, as a club remix of *Pepas* shook the entire room. That's when a five-foot-eight, sharp-browed guy from Molly's group leaned over and introduced himself.

He had that perfectly groomed look, thick brows, messy-but-intentional hair, a silver chain resting exactly where it should, like he'd mapped out his angles before leaving the house. His smirk said *trouble*, but the fun kind. The *let's-get-a-drink-and-spill-everything* kind.

He leaned in, yelling over the music, "I'm Nadeem, by the way. I love your vibe."

"Omg thanks, I'm Bella."

"Who'd you come here with??"

"Myself!"

He physically recoiled in the most dramatic, fabulous way.

"OMG. Stop. I can't. That's so iconic."

We hugged. He pulled me back just slightly, squinting at me like he was unlocking a secret.

"Wait. Are you a Cancer?"

I pulled my sunglasses down just enough to look him in the eyes. "How'd you know?"

"*Bitch*, me too. Want a shot?"

And just like that, we became instant best friends. We spent the rest of the night taking shots of Jäger, dancing under strobe lights at Heaven until the music stopped and the lights came up at 3 a.m.

But I wasn't tired. And neither was Nadeem. I mean, I'd only been out for, like, three hours, hardly a full night's work.

That's when he looked at me and said, "Alright. Next stop: Fire."

Obviously, I said yes.

Apparently, Fire was where most of the gays ended up after Heaven. Ironic, but honestly, kind of fitting. We hopped on a night bus, our ears ringing from the club, making our way across the city like we'd done this a thousand times before.

The energy in Fire was next level. But by 6 a.m. as the sun started to rise, the birds began to chirp, and I'd had my fair share of let's just say *memorable* encounters, I knew it was time to call it a night. Nadeem and I looked at each other, both slightly delirious, and agreed we should probably head home.

I knew from that moment on that Nadeem wasn't just a one-night friend. We didn't exchange long stories about our childhoods. We didn't talk about our five-year plans. But somehow, in those few hours, we became each other's person. From that night forward, we started doing everything together— spending our weekends hopping around the city, saying yes to whatever the night offered. He was the kind of friend who turned last-minute plans into the best memories. Who could hype you up with one look, one song, one shared glance form across the dance floor.

It still amazes me how quickly someone can go from stranger in flashing lights to someone you can't imagine your life without.

That's the thing about friendships built while you're in motion— they form fast, but that doesn't make them any less real. In fact, sometimes they're the ones that stick the most. They see you through change, homesickness, and joy. Nadeem and I were both floating through something at the time, and somehow, we became anchors for each other.

I had finally stopped doubting if I was being invited to things just out of pity. I was building and forming real friendships with people just like Molly and Nadeem. Friends who would become my people. People who made London feel a little less foreign and a lot more like home.

It was such a good feeling. Because, honestly, I had been really lonely when I first moved. I tried to do the right things. Taking walks, treating myself to solo dinners, buying the overpriced cookie in the café window just because it looked insane. But most nights, I ended up in my room, scrolling through old photos and videos, missing everything and everyone I had left behind.

I questioned myself constantly.

Had I made a mistake leaving them?

Should I have just moved to Chicago, where most of my college friends had ended up?

Why did I feel the need to be different—to prove something by doing this on my own?

I'd text my 20-person friend group back home, saying how much I missed them. I'd call my two best girls, Lindsey and Mandy, and tell them how badly I wished they were here. I was so caught up in the nostalgia that I didn't leave room to notice what was forming right in front of me.

I hadn't considered that there were new friendships waiting for me here too. Ones that could be just as meaningful. I just had to be willing to see them.

And then, right on cue, only a week after meeting Nadeem came Jason.

Jason and I had a mutual friend back in Nebraska, but somehow our paths had never crossed until we both ended up in London for grad school. What are the odds? Two Midwesterners connected by accident in one of the biggest cities in the world.

Jason was impossible not to love. He had that all-American look, blonde hair, blue eyes, sharp jawline, dimples for days, and a kind of easy charm that made everyone around him feel like their best self. But beneath his glow was someone grounded, loyal, and always game for whatever came next.

He was effortlessly honest and refreshingly unfiltered. The kind of person who made you feel instantly safe just by being himself. Jason and I would laugh until our stomachs hurt, validating each other's most irrational thoughts without hesitation. No topic was off limits, no judgment ever passed. It was the kind of friendship where you could be ridiculous, vulnerable, and brutally honest all at once.

We met on Halloween night, and from that moment on, we were glued. He became my go-to after a long day of classes, my hype man, my safe space. The kind of friend who says yes to everything because he believes every moment is worth showing up for.

While I started spending my days with both Jason and Nadeem, I slowly started building a friendship with Kat.

Kat and I were in the same master's program, but only saw each other a couple days a week. I was usually with Jason and Nadeem, and Kat stuck close with her flat mates. But gradually, we started hanging out more. A shared post-class lunch here, a drink at our school's pub there.

She's wicked smart (as any true Boston gal should be), sharp-witted, and somehow always five steps ahead in a conversation without ever making you feel like you're behind. One minute we'd be deep in it talking politics, systemic injustice, the absolute madness of the world, and the next, we'd be in full hysterics over our latest horrible Hinge dates.

Kat has this ability to hold space for both. The heavy and the hilarious. The existential spiral and the outfit check. And that balance became such a comfort to me. She was the kind of friend who made you feel smarter by being around her, but also never let things get too serious for too long. She was lively, insightful, and completely, unapologetically herself.

In just a few short months, I had become a completely new version of myself—one that was shaped in large part by the people I had begun to surround myself with. Nadeem, Jason, and Kat loved me for exactly who I was. And that had to be the missing piece of the person I was becoming.

But it wasn't just in the laughter and the good nights out that I realized how deeply these friendships mattered. It was in the worst moment of my year in London.

It was International Margarita Day, and I had just wrapped a long day of classes. Naturally, I texted everyone to celebrate this very important holiday.

I sent Jason a message during class:

"It's Margarita Day…" with a screenshot of a free margarita deal I'd found from one of the many restaurants I was subscribed to.

"Fuck yeah," he replied. "Pregame at mine? Hahaha."

My yes-man. See? Always down for any and everything.

I headed over to his place once classes ended. It was me, Jason, and his roommate Quinn, pregaming with tequila in honor of our beloved margaritas.

We tubed to the restaurant that was offering the 2-for-1 margarita deal and spent a few hours drinking, eating tacos, and dancing to the bar's reggaeton music. And after a few rounds, I parted ways and started the familiar journey home.

I FaceTimed G on my walk from the tube station to my flat, chatting as I always did, just to keep me company and wish her a Happy Margarita Day.

The route was simple: cross one street, cut through the park. I'd taken it dozens of times. Walking through the park shaved two minutes off the trip, so I always did it.

I noticed three people walking behind me as I entered the darkness, leaving behind the lit-up streets, but I didn't think much of it. I was a little tipsy, mid-conversation, finally feeling at ease in my new city.

Until suddenly, I wasn't.

The three drew closer. Two of them, dressed in black, peeled off and disappeared into the trees. The third was a tall girl, also dressed head to toe in black, who walked directly up to me and grabbed my jacket.

"Is this new or old edition?" She demanded.

I stopped walking, G still on FaceTime.

"What?" I asked, confused.

She tugged harder. "Your jacket. Is this a new or old edition?" She repeated, her British accent thick, her eyes fixed on me through a black surgical mask.

"I don't know. It's my friends," I said, pulling back. Jason had lent me his black North Face before I left his flat.

Then she looked down and noticed my phone.

"Turn off your camera."

"No," I said. "I'm talking to my sister."

Her grip tightened.

"You don't want this to get mad."

"What?" I started to say until she pulled out a knife.

She didn't wave it. She didn't yell. She just pointed it to my face—quiet, intentional. "You don't want this to get mad. Turn off your camera or I'll stab you in the face."

I froze. My sister was still on the line.

"Don't hang up, Bella," she said. "Stay on."

But I couldn't move. I couldn't breathe. And then she reached out, grabbed my phone, ended the call, and demanded my passcode.

Still holding onto my arm, she opened my Notes app and made me type it in.

It happened so fast. My mind couldn't catch up. I just remember standing there, completely frozen, in the middle of a park I walked through every single day.

Then she was gone. She took my phone and ran. The other two emerged from the trees and the three of them sprinted off.

I just stood there.

I started walking. Fast. Not running, because I was afraid they might still be watching. I checked over my shoulder every two seconds. My heart was pounding, but all I could think about was G. I had to get to her. I had to call her back and make sure she was okay, and I had to let her know that I was okay, too.

When I finally made it back to my flat, I spent an hour in my lobby reporting the incident to the police. There wasn't much they could do, and to be honest, they weren't very helpful. I did everything I could to hold myself together while talking with them, forcing myself not to cry, just trying to get through it.

But the second the report was finished, I turned away, grabbed my things, and headed to my room. That's when everything hit.

My hands started shaking, my thoughts were spinning. The tears I had been holding back came fast. My phone was gone, and I had no idea what else they could access or how far the damage would go. I felt violated. Exposed.

But thankfully, I still had my laptop. That tiny lifeline saved me. Through it, I was able to message the people who mattered most. I let G know I was okay. I contacted my family. And slowly, shakily, I began the process of trying to piece myself, and everything else, back together.

I woke up the next morning, still in tears, and realized the people who had taken my phone had somehow hacked into all of my accounts. They drained over $10,000 from my savings, changed every password I'd had for years, and locked me out of my digital life completely. I was safe physically, but I was cracked open in every other way. My sense of stability had been ripped out from under me.

What broke me most was how sad it made me to think a stranger could do this to another human being. The trauma didn't leave room for anger. All I remember thinking was how grateful I was that I had never been in a place where harming someone felt acceptable. It broke my heart.

I thought about how different my own life was. How lucky I was to have people I could call. People who showed up in an instant, no questions asked. Friends who didn't need to be told what I needed; they just knew.

Jason was the first one there. He came over that afternoon, no questions, no expectations. He just sat at my desk chair while I tried to sort out whatever pieces I could. We didn't have to talk about what had happened. He didn't try to fix it. He was just there. And his being there, his steady presence, meant everything.

Later that night, Kat and my other two friends, Lily and Pauline, showed up with a care package. A fuzzy blanket. A bottle of wine. Snacks. Small things but filled with the exact kind of softness I didn't know I needed. It wasn't about the stuff. It was what it said: *We see you. We're so sorry. We're here.*

And in that moment, I realized: these weren't just my friends. These were my people.

Because it's easy to show up when everything's fun. When the drinks are flowing, and the plans are exciting. But what happens when it all falls apart? When you're at your lowest, your most vulnerable, and don't even have the words to explain how wrecked you feel? That's when it matters most.

And they showed up. People who I had only known for a few months.

In the moments that followed, these friendships only deepened. Not a moment was taken for granted, because we all knew how little time we had together. Some of us would stay in the city. Some would leave and come back. Others hadn't figured it out yet, all of us hoping time would just slow down.

We started saying "yes" more to impromptu pub nights, to Sunday markets, to late-night takeout and board games in someone's flat. We showed up for each other in the big ways and the small ones. Every hangout felt a little more golden. Every laugh, a little louder. Even in the mundane, there was meaning, because deep down we knew this wouldn't last forever.

When the end of our year crept closer, the goodbyes started to linger a little longer. We'd promise to see each other again soon, knowing that "soon" could mean months, or even years. And yet, we said it anyway, because we meant it.

Now, with oceans and time zones between us, those friendships look different, but they haven't disappeared. They've just transformed.

I've come to believe that long-distance friendship is one of the purest forms of love there is. It asks for presence without proximity. It asks you to show up in unconventional ways: through voice notes, 2 a.m. texts, spontaneous FaceTime calls, or surprise postcards that arrive just when you need them most.

These are the friends who may not know what your kitchen looks like now, or who you ran into at the grocery store last week, but they know the core of who you are. The ones who knew you when you were becoming. Who held you in the in-between.

Friendships like that ask you to trust in the foundation you built together. To believe that miles can't undo what mattered, that connection isn't defined by how often you see someone but how you truly know them.

I think about my London friends all the time. Nadeem and I, dancing until sunrise, meeting strangers in barbershops at five a.m. Kat, Lily, and Pauline, showing up with a fuzzy blanket and wine, wrapping me in a kind of comfort I hadn't even known I needed. Jason, Alex, and Quinn, our laughter echoing through late-night card games and half-finished cans of beer.

We were each other's constants in a season of change. And now, even from across the world, they still remind me who I was then, who I became because of them. And how lucky I am to have people whose presence lingers, even in their absence.

Long-distance friendships are strange like that. They're full of little griefs. You miss birthdays, casual dinners, the everyday things. But they're also full of something so tender. Because when those people do come back into your orbit, even if it's just for a weekend, it feels like no time has passed. Like you just picked up the thread where you last left it.

That kind of love doesn't fade. It stretches. It travels.

And when you find it, you hold onto it, tight.

Because these are your postcards—snapshots of love and light from the people who helped you grow, even if you no longer live in the same frame.

Chapter 8: Mundane Magic

Dear Reader,

So much of life is spent waiting for the big moments, the milestones, the trips we dream about or the events we circle on our calendars. We assume those are the experiences that will make life feel meaningful.

But lately, I've come to realize that some of the most memorable and grounding moments don't come with much notice at all. They show up in the form of everyday routines and passing moments we often overlook. A home-cooked meal with your family after a long week. A walk around the neighborhood with your dog. Sitting on a park bench, watching people pass by—each one absorbed in their own world, carrying their own story.

This chapter is about those kinds of moments. The ones we usually label as "ordinary," but that, when noticed fully, turn out to be extraordinary. There's a kind of magic in the repetition of everyday life—in the simple act of being present for what's right in front of us.

Often, it's not about what we're doing, but how we're experiencing it. The way we see something and the way we feel it can be entirely different. Paying attention to the small things is, in itself, a form of gratitude. It's a way of saying I'm here. This matters. Life doesn't have to be loud or impressive to be beautiful. Sometimes, it's the gentle, grounding things, that remind us we're alive. And that is a gift.

So, if you've ever found yourself wondering whether your life is exciting enough or feeling stuck in a stretch of "nothing special," this chapter is for you.

Because sometimes the most extraordinary moments are the ones we don't even realize we're living until they're gone.

***

It was one of our last days in Australia. Three weeks of driving up the coast of the land down under had left G and me with sun-kissed skin, fresh tattoos, and a plethora of emotions that would leave a lasting imprint on how we see the world. From Sydney to the Gold Coast, Melbourne to Byron Bay, we soaked in a country known for its laid-back culture, sweeping beaches, and effortlessly active way of life. We started and ended our trip in Sydney, returning to the boys we'd traveled with through Italy and collecting new lifelong friends along the way.

But what stayed with us as much as the landscapes were the people who filled them. Everywhere we went, Australians seemed to carry a confidence in how they moved through their lives. Unhurried yet intentional, grounded yet open. There was an ease to the way they approached work, leisure, connection, even strangers like us, as if life wasn't meant to be conquered but participated in. It wasn't the same brand of ambition we'd grown up around in the U.S., nor the polished pace we'd seen in parts of Europe. But it wasn't opposite either. It was simply different, its own kind of logic, and it made G and me rethink how people, people just like us, build meaningful lives thousands of miles away.

Our friend Callan had lent us his big white work van for the day so we could explore parts of Sydney we hadn't seen yet. By then, I'd grown fairly comfortable with Australian road laws, driving on the other side of the road and all that. And despite a small "scratch incident" in a parking garage in Surfers Paradise, I had convinced Callan, G, and, most importantly, myself that I was fully capable of handling a tradie van.

If you've ever been to Australia—or even just met an Australian—you've probably encountered at least one person who works in the trades. It's something I genuinely admire about their society. They offer real alternatives to university straight out of high school, embracing the value of skilled work in a way that many Western cultures insist must be replaced by a college degree. So, when you meet an Aussie tradie, it's never a surprise.

Sparkies, or electricians, are my personal favorite. But really, any tradie will do. There's just something about men who are good with their hands.

As G and I set off in Callan's van, we laughed at the absurdity of it all—two American girls in a giant white work van, driving on the left side of the road, in one of the world's most iconic cities. I mean, what could go wrong?

And yet, somehow, it all worked out. I put my doubts aside and managed to get us safely around Sydney for one of our final adventures. We even snapped a few pictures in and around the van to send to Callan. He replied:

"Ahhh, I can't believe I'm trusting yous with this. Have fun!"

Our destination was the infamous Bondi Beach—Sydney's most iconic coastal neighborhood, packed with tourists, boutique shops, sunburnt backpackers, and unreal views. Bondi has a reputation, and it more than lives up to it.

It's the beach you see on postcards and in travel vlogs—the one everyone insists you *have* to visit while you're in Sydney. And they're not wrong. It's stunning. The water looks Photoshopped, the waves crash with theatrical precision, and the people look like they've walked straight out of a surf documentary or an activewear campaign. We were excited to lean all the way into the Bondi fantasy.

Before heading to the beach to catch a few more rays, we ducked into a burger shop to cool off. We ordered shakes, slid into a table, and let the A/C bring us back to life. And while we sat there, waiting for our number to be called, G and I naturally slipped into something we've always done: we watched people.

G and I are both people-watchers. We come by it honestly.

It's a kind of ritual between us, a stillness we fall into without even trying. When the world slows down around us, we slip into the simple, but sacred act, of paying attention.

Kids spend years studying their parents without even realizing it. Absorbing how they speak, how they laugh, how they move through a room. You inherit their expressions, their pacing, their weird little phrases that come out of your mouth years later and catch you by surprise. And then someone says, "You are so your mom," or "That is exactly something Dad would do," and suddenly the connection makes sense. They live in you.

Sometimes I wonder how much of that is nature and how much is nurture. How much of our curiosity was coded into us from the start, and how much came from years of listening to our mom analyze human behavior or watching our dad read people from the bench with startling precision. Sometimes I think we were born this way. Other times, I'm convinced we were simply raised in a house where trying to understand people was part of our daily routine. Maybe it's a mix of both. Maybe that's why it feels less like a habit and more like something ingrained in us.

As a kid, you don't really know what to make of that. As a teenager, it makes you roll your eyes and swear you'll never become your parents. But as an adult? There's something oddly comforting about it. Like being part of a pattern you didn't even know you were following.

With a psychologist for a mom and a judge for a dad, it's no surprise that my siblings and I developed a sort of innate fascination with people—their stories, their behavior, or the small things they do when they think no one is paying attention. It wasn't just dinner table conversation. It was everyday life.

We were the kids who asked too many questions. Who wanted to know why people did the things they did. We learned early on that tone, body language, and the pauses in between said just as much, if not more, than the words themselves.

Humans, like all animals, are social creatures. We're wired to connect, to observe, to mirror, to make meaning out of shared experience. People-watching isn't just a pastime, it's instinct. It's how we make sense of the world and our place in it.

So now, as adults, G and I still find ourselves watching. Not in a nosy way. More like being curiously attuned to the world around us. Catching glimpses of conversations. Noticing a nervous twitch or a shared glance. Wondering what just happened, or what's about to.

There's something grounding about it. Something steadying about being still long enough to really notice who people are when they're simply existing.

And that's exactly what G and I were doing in the burger shop that day. Sitting across from each other in silence, sipping our shakes, one leg crossed over the other in almost perfect mirror image. I circled my ankle absently, eyes drifting around the room, both of us waiting for our number to be called.

And in that stillness, we watched.

At the table next to us sat an Australian family of four: a mom, a dad, and two young kids with sandy hair and ketchup on their cheeks. The kids were asking questions that only children can get away with.

"Mummy, why does this sauce taste different here than at home?" One of them asked, holding up a fry mid-bite.

"Because this place doesn't use the dodgy stuff," the dad replied with a grin. "It's the real deal, mate."

The younger one chimed in, eyes wide. "Can we go for a swim after this?"

"If you finish your chips, we'll head down to the beach," the mom said, smiling as she wiped her hands on a napkin. "But only if you don't have a full belly of milkshake."

"Aw, but it's *so* yum," the kid groaned, pulling on his straw dramatically.

Their parents answered everything with that uniquely Aussie blend of practicality and warmth. Direct, but never dismissive. They met curiosity with attention. The whole interaction was so simple, so unremarkable on the surface. But in that moment, it felt like watching something whole and honest.

No one was in a rush. No one was half-scrolling through a phone or disengaging from the moment. It was just a family, eating burgers on a Thursday, being there with each other. Simple. Ordinary. And, somehow, beautifully extraordinary.

G and I sat quietly at our table, listening in, sharing small smiles every so often without saying a word. We stayed like that for a while, watching the ebb and flow of strangers coming and going, staff weaving between tables, the restaurant settling into its midday rhythm.

Eventually the shakes were gone, the A/C had cooled us enough, and the sun outside was calling us back. We tossed our cups, stepped into the brightness, and crossed the busy road toward the beach.

From a distance, Bondi looked like it had been sprinkled with confetti—groups of people scattered everywhere, tiny clusters of color and movement. It was a little too crowded for our liking, so we chose a patch of grass on a hill overlooking it all.

We sat propped up in our swimsuit cover-ups, letting the breeze skim over our sun-warm skin as we took everything in. I pulled out my phone and opened the playlist we'd built together over the trip—songs that had slowly become the soundtrack to the movie we were living in. Some were old favorites that felt newly relevant; others were songs passed down from people we'd met along the way.

And, like clockwork, we were back to people watching.

It was a perfect day. Just the two of us sitting on a hill in Australia, watching a world so far from our own unfold in front of us. Both of us sharing the same experience but feeling it internally in our own way; parallel, yet personal.

An older couple passed in front of us, each pushing a stroller. Probably grandparents, we assumed, out giving the parents a break. There was something tender in the way they moved. They were unhurried and practiced, but more relaxed than if they'd been doing this for the first time. I imagine there's a different kind of love that comes with being a grandparent. The gift of having done it once, and now getting to do it again—not with pressure, but with presence. To witness the start of life all over again, and to know just how fast it all goes.

"Life just feels so different here," I said, tugging my knees to my chest, both of our eyes still following the couple as they slowly made their way down toward the sand.

"I know. I've been having so many revelations about life, it's kind of overwhelming," G replied.

"Same," I said. "And I feel like I was having some of these realizations in Europe too, but it just feels... different here."

"Right? It's like people *know* how to live here. They go through the motions, but they're actually present. Existing *fully*, not just existing."

Despite being my younger sister, I've always admired G's wisdom. There's something about the way she sees the world—soft, curious, perceptive—that has always felt older than her age. She's the kind of person who thinks before she speaks, listens with her whole self, and can disarm you with a single, profound observation that somehow captures what you've been trying to untangle for weeks.

I've leaned on her more times that I can count. Not just as my sister, but as my best friend, a sounding board, and, in many ways, a mirror. And while I joke that she gets it all from me, the truth is her perspective grounds me. She has this way of gently pulling me back when I start spiraling into things that don't matter.

Her outlook is rare. A mix of realism and hope, honesty and empathy. It's not performative. It's steady. And being around her makes me want to see the world a little more like she does.

When the couple with the strollers had finally passed, G broke the silence again.

"I was thinking about this conversation I had with Trey the other day," she said, shifting her weight slightly, legs stretched out in front of her. "I was standing in the shower, just processing everything he said. He's really into real estate right now, all about building his future, which is fine. Great, even. But he kept talking about his *purpose.* Saying if someone doesn't know what their life's purpose is, they're doing it wrong."

I looked over, eyebrows raised slightly, already bracing for where this was going.

"Then he asked me what *my* purpose was," she continued, "and said if I couldn't figure it out, he didn't know if he could keep seeing me."

"What?" I blinked. "Wait, *what?*"

"Right?" She laughed. "At first, I was obviously offended. Because, like… what the fuck? But then I started thinking about it more. And I realized that our only real purpose is to live."

"Wait. Say that again," I said, my brain still catching up to those words.

"Our only purpose is to live."

I leaned back, letting her words settle.

"Damn," I finally said. "Yeah. That's it."

I stretched out on the grass, sunglasses on, eyes closed, letting the sun wash over me. Thinking about how the people around us— the families, the couples, the kids, the grandparents, were all just doing exactly that. Living. Not chasing some grand cosmic purpose. Not performing their way toward meaning. Just showing up for their own lives in whatever small, quiet way that made sense to them.

Trey's questions to G, and his take on what it means to have a life's "purpose", weren't unfamiliar. It wasn't the first time I'd heard someone frame life through that kind of lens. The idea that we're all supposed to have some grand mission, a clearly defined *why* for our existence, is everywhere. And to be fair, it's not unreasonable. When we're only given one life to live, of course we're going to try and make sense of it. Of course we're going to ask the big questions. What am I here for? Am I doing it right? Shouldn't there be more?

It's natural for us as humans—social, conscious, meaning-seeking creatures—to want to assign significance to the things we do. To hope our days add up to something bigger. But sometimes, the pursuit of purpose becomes a pressure. Like we're falling behind if we haven't figured it all out yet. Like simply living, simply being, isn't enough.

But what if it is?

Moving back in with your parents in your 20's, especially when it's a healthy, loving environment, feels less like a regression and more like a rare opportunity. You're old enough now to notice things you couldn't before. Old enough to see your family not just as the backdrop of your childhood, but as individuals living full, layered lives of their own.

For me, it was like being a fly on the wall in a life I once lived at the center of. My parents are best friends. They've raised five kids, built careers, and weathered seasons of chaos and change. And now, in this stage of life, with no more kids to shuttle to activities or pack lunches for, they just... live. They still work full time. They still fold laundry and cook dinner and bicker in that familiar, harmless way. But they also take long walks together. They laugh. A lot. They're present. And even though they know I'm there, it often feels like I'm just observing from the sidelines.

They love watching TV series together—it's become part of their routine. Mom gets home from work, sometimes carrying takeout, other times stepping into the smell of something home cooked by Dad. Whoever's around that night sits down at the table, no matter how casual the meal. We check in on each other's day, swap updates, laugh about some ridiculous story from years ago that always seems to resurface at the right time.

Then comes the show. Usually some wild docu-series or reality show where they each pick out their favorite characters and decide who's more dramatic. They settle into their usual spots on the couch, cuddle up like they haven't been married for over 25 years, still finding comfort in the closeness.

Sometimes I join them. Sometimes I just watch from the other room. But either way, I'm always grateful to witness it.

Because there are the moments—the small, and the ordinary— that remind me of what G said on that hill in Australia. That maybe the whole point isn't to chase purpose but to live. That maybe the magic of life isn't found in the peaks but in the pauses. So much of life's beauty live in the parts of life we're conditioned to overlook. And when we came home, that's what stayed with me the most—the way Australia taught us to slow down, to move with intention, to see the world through a kinder lens. There's something about the Australian way of life that makes you notice what truly matters. It's not about doing more; it's about being more awake to the life already in front of you.

Bringing that back to the States has been its own kind of awakening. Life here moves fast—sometimes too fast. We fill our schedules, chase achievements, measure ourselves against timelines that were never ours to begin with. But when I think back to those days on the coast, to the grandparents pushing strollers, the family in the burger shop, to the simple joy of just being, I'm reminded that we get to choose how we move through the world. We get to decide what we honor, what we hold, what we slow down enough to feel.

And the truth is, we're only given one life. One chance to build something worth remembering. So let it be a life full of wonder. Ask questions. Stay curious. Learn from people whose ideas and opinions stretch your own. Love. Love unconditionally, fiercely, courageously. Appreciate the people who make your world feel fuller. Hold your friends and family close; we are not we are without them. And always, always tell someone you love them. You never know which day will be your last—or which day will be theirs.

So live. Not perfectly, not performatively, but fully. Because the magic is already here, tucked inside the ordinary. And that, more than anything, is worth paying attention to.

Chapter 9: The Shape of Our Dreams

Dear Reader,

We all grow up with dreams. Big, wild, untamed visions of who we might become. When we are young, dreams feel limitless. We want to be astronauts, ballerinas, artists, explorers, and storytellers. We imagine ourselves traveling the world, creating, building, discovering. No one tells us, in those early years, that dreams often come with a price tag.

But somewhere along the way, reality enters the picture. Rent is due. Bills stack up. Careers demand stability, and responsibilities rearrange our priorities. And suddenly, the dreams we once held so closely start to feel like distant, impractical luxuries.

So we begin to wonder: Do we have to choose? Can we chase what sets our soul on fire while still building a life that sustains us? Or is the pursuit of a dream reserved only for those with the privilege to risk it all?

I find myself asking theses same questions. My current dream is to travel the world and write. To wake up in unfamiliar cities, to fill pages with the stories of places and people I have yet to meet. But can I do that and still provide for myself? Can I turn passion into something sustainable, or will I have to tuck it away in exchange for security?

And more importantly, what really stops us from going after what we want? Fear? Expectations? The belief that our dreams are indulgences rather than necessities?

This chapter is for anyone who has ever wrestled with these questions. For the dreamers who have been told to be realistic, and for the realists who still feel the pull of something more. Because maybe the answer isn't about choosing between dreams and survival. Maybe it's about learning how to build a life that makes space for both.

***

Growing up, I looked up to the adults in my life, convinced they had everything figured out. They had the job, the house, the family—the markers of success that seemed inevitable, almost scripted. That was life in the suburbs. Everyone you knew lived in a similar house on a similar street, surrounded by families who mirrored your own. It was a bubble, one so complete that anything outside of it felt distant, almost unreal.

You didn't question the blueprint because it was all you had ever known. The milestones unfolded in predictable order, a rhythm of life that was steady and secure. And for a long time, I thought that was the only way life was meant to be.

When I heard stories of people traveling, it was always about the destinations of perfect beaches, exclusive resorts, postcard-worthy moments. It wasn't about the experience of leaving, of stepping outside the unfamiliar and letting the world change you. Travel was framed as an escape, not a way of life. People took vacations, but they always returned to their routines, to their perfectly manicured lawns and two-car garages, to the sense of stability that had been ingrained in us from childhood.

It wasn't until high school that my bubble slowly began to expand. I started volunteering at women's shelters, nursing homes, and childcare centers, stepping into spaces that felt unfamiliar, yet transformative. For the first time, I was seeing a world beyond my own, one that challenged everything I had taken for granted. It was uncomfortable, but it awakened parts of me I never knew existed.

I would sit and listen to the women in the shelters, their voices that told stories of survival, resilience, and hope.

I would observe life in the nursing homes, watching as time slowed, as people faced the quiet reality of their final chapters, some surrounded by loved ones, others left to navigate the end alone.

I would spend time with children who had seen an unfair amount of hardship in their short lives—kids who, more than anything, just needed a little bit of love, a hand to hold, someone to remind them they mattered.

These moments changed me. They cracked open the edges of the world I thought I understood and showed me just how much more there was to see. For the first time, I questioned whether the dream I had built for myself was really mine, or if I had simply inherited it, unquestioned.

I decided I would become a changemaker, dreaming of a world that was faced with less suffering and more compassion. So, upon graduating high school, I chose to pursue a degree in social work—a profession dedicated to confronting injustices and addressing the challenges that plague our communities, both locally and globally. Before, I had seen success as a stable job, a home, a family. But now, I began to wonder if success could mean something else. Maybe it meant creating impact, challenging systems, helping people find hope. Maybe my dream wasn't changing, it was just finally coming into focus.

I became aware of the privileges I held simply because of the color of my skin and the family that raised me. With that realization came a deep commitment to helping those in need in any way I could. Yet, I wrestled with an unsettling thought: did I enjoy helping others for the right reasons? Or was it driven by guilt and shame for the privileged life I had been given?

I wrestled with the idea that dreams, for some, are luxuries, while for others, they are survival. Could I really claim to be a changemaker if my ability to dream at all came from a place of privilege?

The more I thought about it, the more I realized the weight of that question. For many, survival takes precedence over dreaming. The ability to envision a different future, to aspire to something beyond immediate needs, is itself a privilege. I had the luxury of wondering what my purpose was, of seeking fulfillment beyond necessity. But what about those whose dreams are dictated by circumstances—those who dream not of passion or adventure, but of stability, safety, and basic human dignity?

I began to see the barriers that stood between so many people and their dreams. Poverty, systemic oppression, lack of access to education, generational trauma—forces that had the power to shrink a person's world before they even had the chance to imagine something bigger. While I had the freedom to choose between paths, for many, the path was chosen for them before they could even step forward.

This realization didn't lessen my desire to be a changemaker, but it did force me to reconsider what it truly meant. Was change about following my own passions, or was it about dismantling the barriers that kept others from being able to dream at all? Could I justify my own ambitions without using them to uplift those who had been denied the same opportunities?

For the first time, I understood that dreaming wasn't just about personal fulfillment. It was about access, about equity, about creating a world where more people had the freedom to dream at all. And that understanding changed everything.

As my college years flew by, I found myself increasingly overwhelmed by a question that hovered in the back of my mind: Where could I make the greatest impact? Would it be at the micro level, working one-on-one with individuals to help them navigate their struggles? At the community level, driving change that could uplift entire groups? Or at the macro, policy level, where laws and systems, often created without the voices of those they affect, shape the realities of individuals, families, and communities? Each path felt urgent, necessary, and deeply interconnected. But how could I choose just one?

It wasn't until I started traveling that my definition of being a changemaker expanded into something I had never expected. The more of the world I saw, the more I realized that change wasn't just about solving problems, it was about connection.

Meeting people from different cultures, learning about our differences and discovering our similarities, filled me in a way I hadn't anticipated. I had spent so much time feeling overwhelmed by the world's injustices, unsure of where to start. But in seeing the world, I found something even greater than the frustration. I found hope.

Inspired by the people I met, I started writing and blogging about my experiences. I shared stories, names, pictures, and the adventures, whether they lasted one night or four, that had shaped my perspective. These weren't just fleeting encounters; many of these people are still in my life today, scattered across continents, connected through social media. Over time, I began receiving messages from strangers, people thanking me for my words, for offering something they, too, could reflect on. Some sought advice on traveling solo, others asked how to explore the world on a budget.

Without realizing it, I had become a changemaker in a way I had never envisioned—one that wasn't solely focused on injustice and struggle, but on growth, connection, and shared human experience.

Change, I realized, didn't always have to come from fighting against something. Sometimes, it could come from celebrating what already connects us.

The more I leaned into the path of writing, wandering, and connecting, the more I noticed just how differently dreams can look for everyone. I'd scroll through social media and see friends, both old and new, getting married, settling down, announcing pregnancies, building the life they had always envisioned. A life rooted in stability, in family, in tradition. And I'd pause, not out of envy, but out of awe. Because as beautiful as their dreams were, I couldn't quite comprehend them—couldn't imagine myself in their shoes.

It was also a curious thing to me that the people closest to me were walking paths much more like mine. While the friends I saw on social media were getting engaged, planning weddings, and building families, their closest circles seemed to be doing the same. Meanwhile, the people I was surrounded by, my closest confidants, the ones I traveled alongside were, like me, in no rush to settle. They were chasing freedom, adventure, growth.

It made me wonder: Do we choose the path because it's what we want, or because it's what we've seen? Do we gravitate toward people whose dreams mirror our own? Or do our dreams slowly begin to reflect the company we keep?

It felt like a quiet sorting had happened, not out of exclusion but evolution. Maybe we surround ourselves with people who validate the life we're creating, who make us feel less alone in the choices we've made. And maybe that's why, to me, marriage and family feel like someone else's language—beautiful, but not one I speak fluently. At least not yet, not in my current dreams.

I thought about two men I had once dated—each one living on opposite ends of a spectrum I couldn't seem to reconcile with myself.

The most recent was perhaps the most non-committal person I had ever met. He worked odd jobs, booked last-minute flights to random countries, and always seemed to be chasing the next spontaneous adventure. From the very beginning, he made it clear that what we had was casual—strictly physical, no strings, no expectations.

"So…would you ever go on a date with me?" I asked one night, lying in his bed. I already knew the answer, but I wanted to hear it anyway.

He smirked. "This is a date."

I laughed, playing along. "You know what I mean. Like… a drink at a bar, in public. Nothing serious."

"Yeah, I don't know. Maybe."

Maybe, meant no. And I knew then not to bring it up again.

As much as I admired his honesty, there was still a part of me that hoped I might be the exception. That somehow, I'd be the one who made him want to stay. We were so similar—restless, curious, addicted to movement, and I convinced myself I could play the part of the cool girl who didn't want more.

I started to mirror his energy, echoing his language, dropping casual hints like I wasn't actually hoping he'd change his mind.

"If I had a remote job, I'd be in a new city every six weeks," I said once, hoping he'd see I had similar desires to his.

"That would be so sick," he replied. "I know people who could do that and just don't. Total waste."

I told him how cool I thought it was that he was flying to Costa Rica for a few days just because the flight was cheap. Or how wild it was that he agreed to run a half marathon in Texas with a friend, even though he hadn't trained.

Because I, too, chased adventure. I, too, wasn't looking to settle. At least, that's what I told myself.

But beneath that surface, there was another truth I wasn't ready to admit: a longing for something more.

Not "more" in the white-picket-fence, mortgage and matching-dog-bowls kind of way. But more as in real. Something raw. With presence. I wanted to be met emotionally, intellectually, and spiritually, not just passed through like a layover.

I didn't need a label. But I wanted depth. Intention. I wanted someone to ask real questions and wait for the real answers. To see past the image I'd curated so carefully—the one who was always down for adventure, always cool, always unbothered, and notice the parts of me that weren't always easy to carry.

I wanted something that didn't disappear when the sun came up. Something that didn't have to pretend it wasn't craving connection just as much as I was. Even if it didn't last forever, I wanted it to still matter.

And that's when I thought of James, the boy I dated before moving to London. The one who checked every box. He had the job, the apartment downtown, the steady life that looked, on paper, exactly like the stability I was supposed to want.

"I just want to travel the world," I'd tell him, caught up in my daydreams. "See as much as I can in the short time we have on this earth."

He'd nod. "Yeah, I get that. I want that too. But, like… when I'm in my 30s and financially stable."

I wanted to shake him.

Didn't he see it? That now was the time? That we didn't have mortgages or kids or decades of routine tying us down? That adventure isn't something you postpone until life feels more convenient? It's something you chase when the pull is so strong it drowns out everything else.

And yet, I also understood him. That scared me. There was a part of me that longed for what he represented: stability, routine, the kind of love that doesn't demand you uproot everything to feel held. A part of me wanted to want that life. To find peace in the ordinary. But another, louder part knew I'd suffocate in it.

And I felt bad for him sometimes, because he never really got the full version of me. By the time we met, Europe had already changed me. Those first three weeks opened my eyes to a whole new world, and I couldn't pretend I didn't feel it. I was already craving more. More movement, more possibility. And without fully realizing it, I had one foot out the door long before I applied for the program in London. He walked into my life right as I was already dreaming of somewhere else.

So when I got my acceptance letter for my master's program, I was ecstatic. It was the kind of news I needed to take a step toward my new dreams of seeing as much of the world as I could.

It was Valentine's Day, and I was sitting in my car in the P.F. Chang's parking lot, dreading another shift at a restaurant that I felt no longer served me. I was tired. Not just physically, but spiritually tired. Tired of carrying trays and pretending I wasn't craving something more. Tired of the predictable rhythms of a life I no longer fit into.

I opened my email, barely expecting anything. And then, there it was: an acceptance letter, congratulating me on my offer to study in London. My hands started shaking. Tears welled up in my eyes. I couldn't believe it. This news was going to change everything.

James was happy for me—proud, even—but we both knew, deep down, that it marked the beginning of an ending.

It was the end of February when we took a trip to the mountains, a belated Valentine's escape. Over dinner, the topic finally surfaced.

"I can't wait to visit you in London," he beamed, smiling. "You'll get to show me around. I'll visit whenever I can."

An unknown feeling came over me. I hadn't fully considered what moving away would mean for us, not until that moment. But once the words were out there, I couldn't ignore the truth: I couldn't imagine being in a relationship when the time came.

"Yeah…" I said hesitantly, taking a sip of my cabernet.

He blinked. "What?"

"I just… I hadn't really thought about it. But honestly? I don't know if that's realistic. It's not like I'm moving to a different state, James. It's a whole ocean. Thousands of miles."

His face tightened. "Then what's the point of being together now if it's going to end?"

I paused. "I like what we have now. London's still months away. Who knows where we'll be by then."

And I meant it. At that point, we'd only been together a few short months. I loved him, and I loved the way our relationship felt: calm, safe, stable. He showed up for me. He was good to me. He made life feel easy.

But as time went on and London drew closer, something became clearer. James loved me, but he didn't see me. Not in the way I needed. He couldn't understand why I wanted to live out of a backpack or sleep in airport terminals just to see a new city. He couldn't grasp why I'd trade security for uncertainty. His world didn't have space for mine.

And mine felt stifled in his.

I was never able to put my full 100% into the relationship after that conversation in the mountains. It settled in the back of my mind. And he had a point, what really *was* the point?

Still, walking away didn't come easy. I kept asking myself if I was making a mistake—if wanting something *more* meant giving up something *good*. James and the other boy I mentioned lived on opposite ends of a spectrum I couldn't seem to reconcile within myself.

One offered stability, the other freedom. One saw a future measured in calendars and paychecks, the other lived moment to moment with no guarantees. And I found myself suspended somewhere between the two aching for a kind of love that didn't require me to choose one version of myself over another.

Not a perfect partner, but someone who saw me. Who could hold both the intensity and the ease. Who could meet me where I was, and not try to mold me into something I wasn't ready to be.

And while I didn't envy the friends getting engaged to their high school or college sweethearts, I still wondered—should that be me? Was I missing something by not wanting what they had? Was there a version of love that didn't come with either/or?

And maybe that's what I was really grappling with. Not just love, but the shape of the life I was building. The shape of my dreams.

Because the truth is, I've spent years trying to fit into versions of myself that were easier to explain. The "chill girl" who doesn't ask for more. The girlfriend who finds comfort in the stable plan.

The adventurer who claims not to need anyone. But none of those identities felt entirely true. And maybe the dream isn't about choosing one over the other. Maybe it's about making room for it all.

Because here I am now traveling around cities I once only imagined, writing words that once felt too bold to say out loud. I've watched my life slowly unfold into something I didn't plan for, but somehow knew I needed. I wake up in new places, I meet people who challenge and change me, and I get to tell stories about it all.

Like the story of Frey.

I met him in Prague, on an ordinary evening that turned out to be anything but. I was sitting alone on the terrace of our hostel, sipping a canned cider and watching everyone else chit-chat around me—strangers colliding, friendships forming in real time.

"Are you enjoying the view?" He asked, his Swedish accent curling around the words with a grin I wasn't expecting.

I raised my drink to him, laughing. "Apparently, yes."

That's how it started. A conversation so easy and effortless it felt like we'd picked it up halfway through, even though we'd just met. He sat beside me, and we talked until the background noise faded. It was talk about the usual things at first—where we were from, where we were headed next, but before long we were down a rabbit role. We started laughing and sharing stories you don't usually tell someone you just met. There was something about the way he listened that made me want to keep talking. And something about the way he spoke back that made me feel he understood me beyond the surface.

We followed the rest of our hostel crew to a funky bar, filled with different themed rooms, but it may as well have been just the two of us. We found a quiet corner, barely touched our drinks, and fell into more conversation that stripped time away.

"Wow, Bella. There's just something about you. It's something in your eyes." He said, both of us staring into each other's eyes.

"Oh, yeah?" I said, widening my eyes even more.

Frey blushed and looked away.

"You can't fall in love with me now, Frey," I carried on. "You leave tomorrow."

And what a shame that was.

When the bar closed and our group filtered back to the hostel in pairs and small clusters, Frey and I headed up to a hill that was tucked behind our hostel. We climbed the stairs and steep hills that eventually led to a piece of grass under some trees. The city was still below us.

It was 3 a.m.

I laid back and rested my head on his chest, the rhythm of his breath steady beneath me. Above us, the branches swayed gently in the breeze, and through them, the ancient skyline of Prague stretched wide—spires and rooftops silhouetted against a sky just beginning to fade from black to soft blue.

"I get so frustrated when I meet someone I connect with so easily, like I do with you," I whispered, afraid that saying it too loud might somehow undo the moment.

"Why's that?" He asked, turning slightly to look at me.

"Because it never lasts. These connections—these beautiful, intense, fleeting things, they're so rare. And yet, when I'm traveling, they happen. But they're always temporary. And I think I'm just tired of things that feel so real disappearing so quickly."

He was quiet, letting it sink in.

"I know you see me," I added. "And understand me. And that's not something I find often. Especially not in my daily life."

"This is your daily life," he said gently, as if offering a truth I had overlooked.

I laughed lightly, then nodded. "Yes, you're right. It is. But I mean the other life with all of the routine and responsibilities back home."

"I understand. But this is your life," he said again. "Don't make it feel smaller just because it feels different."

And that was it. A sentence that has stayed with me ever since.

Because isn't that what we all do? We shrink moments that don't fit neatly into a plan. We downplay the magic if it isn't permanent, tell ourselves it doesn't count unless it leads somewhere unfamiliar. But maybe it's those very moments with the 3 a.m. conversations on a hill in Prague with a Swedish boy you'll never see again that matter most. Maybe they are the blueprint. Maybe they don't exist to fit inside our plans, but to gently, radically reshape them.

Because the shape of our dreams is not fixed. It's fluid. It bends and shifts with the seasons of our lives, with each person who opens a new part of us, with every place that reveals a version of ourselves we hadn't yet met. Some people build their dreams around permanence—roots, rings, routines. Others, like me, build them in motion, in memory, in the wild and unpredictable unfolding of a life that doesn't always make sense on paper, but makes perfect sense to the heart that's living it.

And yet, I know now that none of this is guaranteed. The ability to even ask, *What do I want?* is itself a luxury. I carry that truth with me wherever I go, with gratitude. And I've stopped trying to pretend that I deserve this life more than anyone else. I don't. I'm just lucky enough to be living it. And because of that, I feel a responsibility to honor it. To write it down. To share it. To remind others that there is no one way to dream.

So wherever you are—whether you're starting over, standing still, or chasing something that still feels just out of reach, I hope you remember this: It's never too late to rewrite the blueprint. To expand the shape of your dreams. To believe that your life can still surprise you.

Because it can.

And maybe all it takes is a little courage. A little trust. And a single moment that reminds you of everything that's still possible.

Chapter 10: This Version of You

Dear Reader,

Have you ever looked back on a past version of yourself and thought: who even was that? Not in judgement, but in genuine awe. Like you're flipping through the pages of your own story and suddenly land on a chapter that feels both familiar and impossibly far away.

It's wild how many versions of ourselves we live in one lifetime.

The one where you were fearless.

The one where you were lost.

The one where you were trying so hard to keep it all together.

The one where you finally let go.

Some of those versions are shaped by choice. Others, by circumstance. And some arrive without warning, just a slow change in the way you see the world, or yourself, or the people around you.

I think we all have a moment—maybe several—where something changes. A feeling, a realization, a conversation. Something that makes you pause. Reevaluate. Begin again.

And suddenly, you're not who you were. You become someone new.

Sometimes we leap into the next version of ourselves with excitement and a little fear. Other times, life pushes us, whether we're ready or not. But either way, there's something incredibly human in learning how to start over. How to soften. How to slow down. How to build a life that fits the person we've grown into.

So, as you read, I hope you'll reflect on the versions of yourself that have gotten you this far. The messy ones and the brave ones. The ones you said goodbye to and the ones still waiting for you.

Because we're not meant to stay the same. We're meant to change. To stretch. To evolve. To begin again.

***

My graduate school supervisor challenged me in more ways than one. Each month, we had mandatory check-ins where she'd review my progress on my thesis. These meetings were usually a mix of practical suggestions and pointed feedback—never mean, but always direct. She was the kind of mentor who expected a lot because she believed you were capable of more.

Every time I submitted a draft, it came back to me full of highlights, tracked changes, and giant question marks. One piece of feedback appeared again and again: *"This needs to tell a story."*

At first, I didn't really get it. I was writing an academic thesis, not a novel. I was researching stakeholder responses to a federal guidance document on the clinical use of psychedelic drugs—not exactly bedtime reading. I couldn't understand how I was supposed to create *that* into a story.

But she kept pushing.

Then, about a month before the final version was due, I submitted what I thought was my strongest draft yet. I had edited it carefully, incorporated her notes, and felt like I was finally getting somewhere. I told myself the hard part was over. I thought this draft would only need a few final tweaks.

A week later, I opened her email and felt my stomach drop. Nearly the entire 10,000-word document was highlighted, annotated, and marked up. Whole sections had been circled with notes suggesting I rethink the framing. I stared at the screen in disbelief.

I texted my parents in frustration:

"Supervisor destroyed my draft. I want to cry. I'm so frustrated."

My mom, who's basically been in school her whole life, with four master's degrees and two doctorates to show for it replied with exactly what I needed to hear: "I'll tell you the best advice I got while writing my dissertation: Make the corrections and move forward."

And so, I did. I sat with the edits. Took a deep breath. And went back in.

Slowly, I began to understand what my supervisor had meant all along. A thesis—like anything worth writing—still needs a through-line. A point of view. A beginning, middle, and end. Even in academic work, readers want to understand *why* something matters, *who's* involved, *what's* at stake. They want to feel like they're being taken somewhere, not just handed data.

So, I started telling the story. I threaded together the voices of the stakeholders. I explored their concerns and hopes and framed the guidance document not as a cold bureaucratic policy—but as a piece of something bigger: a shift in thinking, history repeating, and a conversation still unfolding.

It wasn't easy. But it was better. And somewhere in the process of rewriting—not just in polishing the language but learning how to truly shape something into a story—I started thinking about how that applies to more than just a page.

Writing, I've come to realize, isn't the only thing that asks us to tell a story. Life does, too.

Throughout my meetings with my supervisor, little pieces of her life began to surface. Our relationship became more personal and more human. She wasn't just an academic guiding me through edits, she became a mentor. And through the stories she shared, I got a glimpse of just how many lives she'd lived before the one I was witnessing on Zoom.

We found common ground in Colorado, a place we'd both once called home. She told me about her time in the Four Corners region, where she lived as a cowgirl—yes, a literal cowgirl—wrangling horses and working the land that bordered Utah, Arizona, and New Mexico. Later, she would go on to complete a PhD in cultural and medical anthropology in Montreal, eventually becoming a professor of global health in London. Now, here she was as someone I looked up to, meeting with me over video calls in between lectures and research deadlines.

It struck me just how many versions of herself she'd lived through. How one person could contain so many chapters—so many changes in pace, place, and purpose. And while I'd already spent time thinking about the roles we assign to people, this felt different. This wasn't just about the labels we wear; it was about the full evolution of self. The choices, the turning points, the circumstances that shape us into someone new over and over again.

Getting to know my supervisor beyond her title helped me understand what she really meant when she said: *tell a story.* Because that's what we're all doing, every day. Whether we're writing it down or living it in real time. We are stories in motion, becoming new versions of ourselves with each season, each change, each stumble forward.

Now, when someone shares a detail from their past—a glimpse into a life they lived before—I pause. I lean in. I find myself wondering who they were then, and how that version of them still lingers inside. How many more lives might be tucked away in their story, waiting to be shared.

It's something I think about often with my brother, Christian.

If anyone embodies the idea of living multiple lives, it's him. Some I've witnessed. Others, I can only imagine. He's an autodidact in the truest sense: self-taught, self-directed, and always chasing meaning on his own terms. The life he's living now is just the latest chapter in a story full of reinvention, resilience, and reckoning.

For most of my childhood, I didn't even call him Christian. I called him, "Brother." A nickname that stuck after I struggled to pronounce his name as a toddler and somehow lasted until my early teens. He's eight years older than me, and by the time I was really becoming aware of the world around me, Christian had already moved out. He was always somewhere new. Always in motion.

His life stretched across cities and continents—Chicago, Cambodia, Austin, and everywhere in between. And because I was so young, I rarely knew where he was or what exactly he was doing. It was a bit of a mystery. He changed phone numbers constantly, so our best (and often only) form of communication became Facebook Messenger. I'd get a random photo, a meme, or a "what's up Lala" message from some corner of the world, and that was enough to feel connected. Kind of.

But our relationship shifted in the early years of COVID. He had moved back to Denver, and for the first time in a long while, our visits became more consistent. What once was a dynamic of tattling on each other evolved into something more grounded. We stepped into our roles as the eldest siblings—the ones who felt a little more responsible for the other three, who could look back on our own adolescence with just enough distance to laugh about it.

We'd swap stories about our younger siblings, laughing about their teenage antics one minute, turning serious the next and talking about how to support them without overstepping or becoming the know-it-all older siblings we once resisted ourselves.

We talked about Mom and Dad too. About how they were entering a new season of life, one less defined by parenting and more about rediscovering each other. After three decades of raising five kids, the finish line was finally in sight. You could feel their shift. Less carpools and curfews, more breakfasts in bed and shared shows.

Christian and I often circled back to Dad's health. We both carried a worry that everything he had endured—his chronic kidney issues, his genetic heart condition, the heart attacks and strokes—would one day catch up to him. He'd been sick our entire lives, but he always carried it without complaint. Still, there was always this sense that his body was carrying more than it should have to, and that maybe life never really gave him a break.

"He's been parenting for over thirty years," Christian would say, shaking his head with a mix of admiration and disbelief. "It was just me and him for so long. The little bachelor duo bouncing between apartments and surviving on frozen pizzas and drive-thrus."

When my dad was only 25, he was given full custody of Christian, something nearly impossible for a young father to win in the 1990s. He was a full-time law student, struggling himself, but Christian's mom was battling addiction and couldn't safely care for him, and the court recognized the severity of the situation.

Christian and Dad had lived a whole life before the rest of us even existed. A chapter that was theirs alone. My mom entered their lives when Christian was six, expanding their little world. She didn't erase the years he and my dad had weathered together, nothing could. But she became a steady presence, someone who offered warmth, structure, and a different kind of love. The family we would eventually become began to form.

Christian can still name the streets they lived on, describe the exact layout of each apartment, and recall the rhythm of those early days with a clarity that makes them feel tangible. Those times shaped him. They made him independent, observant, and fiercely loyal. Christian has always marched to the beat of his own drum, and proudly so. He's never been interested in doing things the conventional way.

But his path wasn't easy. Like many early lives marked by change and challenge, Christian's story didn't follow a straight line. In his early teens, Christian spent time in group homes—placed there because of behavioral struggles. The system didn't really know what to do with a kid like Christian—brilliant but restless, curious but confrontational, too sharp for his own good.

By sixteen, he had taken the GED and walked away from traditional school altogether. And from that point on, Christian was carving his own way. He didn't just drift, he built. He taught himself everything from philosophy to politics, jumped from city to city, pursued ideas as they came, and met life with both defiance and drive.

At the time, I was old enough to sense something was off, but too young to understand the full picture. I'd catch bits and pieces of adult conversations, feel the tension when his name came up, or notice the quiet worry that settled into my parents' faces. My younger siblings were too little to pick up on any of it. But I did.

Christian had always been the older brother I admired, the one I used to follow around the house, calling him "Brother" like it was his actual name. But then he wasn't around anymore. And slowly, the image I had of him in my mind stopped matching the person I'd hear in passing.

As time went on, Christian became more of a stranger to me. I didn't know where he was most of the time—or who he was. The brother I'd once worshipped had turned into a distant figure I didn't quite recognize, someone whose life was happening somewhere far away from mine, in pieces I couldn't fully put together.

And for a long time, that's just how it was.

But time has a way of circling back. Christian started spending more time in Denver again, and I was in college, coming home for breaks with a little more perspective and a lot more curiosity. The distance between us, once so wide, began to feel a little smaller.

So, when I was home, I looked forward to spending time with him—catching up, trading ideas, gossiping, learning from him. That early sibling bond we had as kids found its footing again but now as adults, with a friendship layered on top.

And just as we were finding our rhythm again, in the fall of 2021, everything changed.

Another wave of COVID had hit the U.S., and Christian got sick. At first, it didn't seem like anything too serious. Maybe it was just a bad case of something that would pass. He was young. Strong. He'd been through harder things in life than a virus.

But within days, he was hospitalized. Then sedated. Then placed into a medically induced coma. Hooked up to machines. Fighting for his life. And he would stay that way for over six weeks.

Most of that time feels like a blur now, likely dulled by the trauma of it all. A survival response, maybe. I was in Madison, Wisconsin, visiting Caleb at the time—a relationship I kept from my parents. They didn't approve of him, and I knew deep down they were right. But still, I made the five-hour drive from Omaha when I could. It wasn't smart, and it certainly wasn't sustainable, but lust can be convincing when you're young and trying to outrun your better judgement.

I was sitting at the edge of his bed when I got the call from my mom. I knew Christian had been sick, but I hadn't been too concerned. He was 29. Healthy and resilient in ways I couldn't always explain but never questioned. I figured he'd bounce back like he always did.

But I could hear it in her voice. This time was different.

"He's going to the ER," she said, her tone controlled and serious. "He's having trouble breathing. They need to monitor his oxygen levels."

"Is it COVID?" I asked.

"Seems like it."

Fucking COVID. Hadn't we all been through enough already?

A year and a half into a global pandemic, and the losses kept piling up. Lives put on hold. Lives lost. Families stretched thin or broken apart. Governments struggling, failing their people. It was a collective grief the whole world had been carrying—but this time, it wasn't a distant headline or a friend-of-a-friend story. This time, it was my brother.

Each day in the ICU brought something new. Some days offered small signs of progress—tiny wins we clung to with cautious optimism. Other days knocked him back, erasing the gains and resetting the clock. It was a slow, unpredictable waiting game. And the hardest part was there wasn't much any of us could do.

We hoped. We prayed. We placed our trust in the medical team who showed up each day to stand by his side because we couldn't stand by him ourselves.

COVID restrictions were still in place. Only one visitor was allowed. And that responsibility fell to Dad.

Every day, he sat at Christian's bedside, dressed head to toe in PPE. Mask, gloves, face shield. Alone in a sterile room full of beeping machines and unanswered questions. Watching. Waiting. Holding his son's hand, even when Christian couldn't hold back.

To keep us informed, and maybe also to stay afloat, Dad began writing daily blog updates. They were factual and full of feeling. A way to keep friends and family in the loop, yes, but also a place for him to put the emotions that had nowhere else to go.

His first journal entry read:

September 27, 2021: "While this is my first journal entry, it is day 12 of Christian's hospitalization at St. Joseph's Hospital in Denver, Colorado and Day 5 in the ICU on a ventilator. To put it bluntly, Christian is fighting for his life against this very real, and very deadly COVID-19. We are in this for the long haul. His status and condition often change daily if not sometimes hourly. His prognosis at this point is guarded and any success is measured in how he does over the next several weeks, not days. We must all be patient and hope for very small milestones of success, i.e. he doesn't get worse. Under the best-case scenarios, he will have a long recovery even after the hospital."

Over time, the daily posts became weekly ones. The days bled together. Progress was slow. Exhaustion crept in.

I was away during most of this time, back in Omaha, finishing school. I knew my parents and siblings were overwhelmed at home, and I struggled being afar.

All I could do was wait. And refresh. And hope.

I didn't let go of my phone, checking the blog updates obsessively. I'd open my Mail app every hour, thumb pulling down on the screen in search of something, or anything, that would offer some clarity.

It had been two weeks of waiting from afar when I was finally able to go home during fall break to be with my family. Restrictions at the hospital had eased slightly since Christian was somewhat stable, and close relatives were now allowed to visit.

And as much as I wanted to see my brother—to hold his hand, to tell him I loved him—I couldn't bring myself to do it. I was terrified to see him like that. I couldn't bear the thought that my last image of him might be one of him unconscious in a hospital bed, hooked up to machines, with a trach in his throat and wires coming out of him like threads holding him together.

At the time, my dad's most recent journal entry was:

October 5, 2021: "Rounds started this morning with "Christian Scipione is a 29 yo with acute respiratory failure due to COVID-19 and has been on a ventilator for 13 days." It's really hard to focus on any other words after hearing that. Christian remains paralyzed and unconscious. His tachycardia appears to increase after longer stints on his stomach. This morning was really tough. I spent of a lot of time staring blankly at his machines and his pictures on the wall. There's only so much you can take staring at him in his current state without breaking down."

His update should have prepared me, but instead it only made everything feel more impossible to face. The decision wasn't easy. I went back and forth for days, unsure if I was doing the right thing. It felt selfish, and it felt protective, and I didn't know which part of me to listen to.

That day, I drove G and Dom to the hospital. My dog Bonnie sat curled on G's lap in the passenger seat with her soft white fur and big brown eyes that could settle anyone's nerves in an instant. G's indie rock playlist played softly in the background.

"I don't know if I can do this, guys," I said, my hands gripping the steering wheel a little tighter than usual.

I've always had a deep appreciation for conversations in the car. Maybe it's the way everyone's looking forward, not forced to meet each other's eyes. Or maybe it's the movement of the road, the familiar noise of tires on pavement, a space that feels removed from everything else.

"I think it would be good for you to see him," G said gently. "I need to see him. I need him to hear me, even if he can't respond, just to know that I'm there."

"I know," I said, my voice tight. "I want that too. But I also know I'll be a wreck if I go in there. And if he…" I paused. "If he doesn't make it, I don't want that to be the last image I have of him in my head."

G didn't respond. She just looked ahead, eyes on the road that stretched in front of us.

Dom sat quietly in the back middle seat, listening but not chiming in. That's just how he is—always tuned in, always absorbing before deciding if and when to speak. Especially in conversations like this, between his two older sisters. He knows when to give space.

"I refuse to believe that he won't make it through this," I said, my voice a little louder than before, like I was trying to will the words into reality. "He's been through too much. I refuse to let COVID take him from us."

My throat tightened. Tears welled in my eyes. I swallowed and kept going.

"If I go in there and see him like that… my mind will spiral. I'll lose it. I know I will. And if I start imagining the worst, I'll start believing it. I can't give up hope. I can't."

Neither of them said anything. The silence sat with us. Not heavy or uncomfortable, but real. Like they both understood I wasn't really talking to them, I was talking to myself. Repeating the lines I needed to hear out loud, trying to convince myself that the decision I was making wasn't just fear in disguise.

A few seconds passed. G shifted slightly in her seat.

"I understand," she said finally. Her voice was calm. Soft.

I dropped them off at the hospital and drove to a nearby park with Bonnie. We found a quiet, shaded spot beneath a tree, and I laid out a blanket while she curled up beside me. I played music from my phone. I played songs that let my thoughts wander without pulling me too far in any direction. I ran my fingers through Bonnie's fur, her breathing slow and warm against my side. I waited for a text from G or Dom to let me know they were ready to be picked up.

An hour or so passed. Maybe more.

I just lay there, staring up at the sky through the branches above, thinking about Christian. About our relationship, the shape of it over the years. About the distance we'd closed and the space that still lingered. I thought about all the lives he's lived—the ones I've known, the one's I've only heard about, and the ones I'll never fully understand.

And I thought about the ones still ahead of him. The chapters yet to be written because there had to be more.

My phone buzzed. A text from G:

"We're ready to go. Can you come get us?"

"On my way," I replied.

The drive home was quiet. And after a few minutes, I asked, calmly, "How was he?"

G let out a small sigh. "It was really hard. I don't blame you for not wanting to see him like that. We played him music. Talked to him. Even though he couldn't respond, I know he felt our presence."

I nodded; my hands steady on the wheel.

"I'm proud of you guys for going," I said. "You're strong."

And I meant it.

After more than fifty days in the hospital, most of them in the ICU, Christian was finally discharged.

He was transferred to a rehabilitation center, back to breathing mostly on his own, the trach removed, his voice slowly returning. For the first time in months, he was able to wear his own clothes again. Sweatpants. A hoodie. The small, ordinary details that made it all feel a little more real.

The progress he made in those final days at the hospital was nothing short of miraculous. The doctors said so. Just weeks earlier, we weren't sure if he would make it. If we would ever hear him laugh again. If he'd see another birthday.

But he did.

And when he was able to speak, he talked about life as a second chance. A do-over. A gift. Soon after, he put those feelings into words.

On December 2nd, 2021, Christian wrote an entry to the same site my dad had been updating loved ones on:

"As I re read every day's log of my stay in the hospital, I'm extremely overcome with emotion. It's a rollercoaster of disbelief, sadness, gratitude, and above all else, relief. I'm happy to report that I am back to living free and

independently with oxygen and assistance only for physical therapy. My doctors and nurses have said frequently how miraculous my recovery has been. At times I'm still a bit unsure of how badly this sickness affected everyone, until I feel the trachea scar on my throat, or the pain in my body that is residual from being in a bed for two months. I cry every time I read these entries, and the outpouring of support everyone gave. I truly have found a new lease on life as I inch closer to my 30th birthday."

Today, Christian lives in Vietnam with his beautiful wife, Meo Meo, where he teaches English and has welcomed their first daughter, Gabriella Rose. A new beginning in every sense. He moved there almost exactly a year after being discharged from the hospital. It was a move that felt like both a leap and a homecoming.

It was his second chance; far from the pressure and expectations of a society that had never quite made space for who he was. A society that failed him in many ways. One he no longer felt he belonged to.

In Vietnam, he found a pace and purpose that fit. And in many ways, he became someone new again.

Another version. Another chapter. Another life.

Because that's what we do. We begin again.

Sometimes with a plan. Sometimes with a push. Sometimes without even realizing it.

We learn to keep going, even when things feel unfamiliar. We carry pieces of our past selves into the lives we're building now, often without noticing how much we've changed until we take a moment to look back.

That's what Christian did. That's what my supervisor taught me. And it's something I keep coming back to—how we're always becoming. Always adjusting, learning, and slowly stepping into whatever comes next.

The lives we've lived before don't disappear. We don't land in one fixed identity or find the final answer, we keep showing up for the process. To be open to shifts. To let ourselves change and to let that change feel okay.

Because every version of you has something to say.

And every version belongs.

So, keep going, keep noticing. Keep telling your story as it unfolds. There's still so much of it left to live.

Part Three: Return and Reclamation

Chapter 11: Vulnerability is Sexy

Dear Reader,

I've never really understood the trend of women calling themselves "man haters" or tossing out lines like "all men are trash." I know where it comes from—the frustration, the heartbreak, the exhaustion of navigating a world that has often minimized and mistreated us. But still, I don't like it. Because it flattens something too complex, too human, to be summed up in a punchline.

I don't hate men. I hate the systems that hurt them and the narrow boxes we've all been shoved into. I hate that boys are told from an early age that strength means silence. That emotions are weakness. That vulnerability is something to be hidden, mocked, or outgrown. I hate that girls are told to take up less space—emotionally, physically, intellectually—so the men around them can feel bigger.

But I also know this: I've seen vulnerability modeled by some of the strongest men I know.

I've watched my dad cry. I've seen my brothers show up for the people in their lives with tenderness and intentionality. I've had male friends call me just to say, "I'm not okay," and mean it. These are not moments of weakness. These are the moments that make me trust them more.

I think of the powerful women in history. Not the ones behind the scenes, but the ones standing right next to the men we were told were leading. Because real leadership, real strength, has always been shared. The most grounded men I've met, straight or queer, have had equally powerful, outspoken, emotionally intelligent women in their lives. Not competing with them but rising with them.

So yes, vulnerability is sexy. So is softness. So is showing up, fully and honestly, for the people we love, and for ourselves.

This chapter isn't a takedown. It's a reckoning. An invitation to rethink what it means to be "strong," and to tell the boys in our lives—and the men they grow into—that there is nothing more attractive than truth, depth, and heart.

✳✳✳

Throughout history, some of the most powerful men have been accompanied—not overshadowed but complemented—by even more powerful women. Women whose strength didn't need to roar to be felt. Women who shaped kingdoms, inspired movements, and challenged the boundaries of their roles long before we had language for feminism.

Coretta Scott King didn't just stand behind Dr. Martin Luther King Jr.; she stood beside him, and after his death, continued fighting for justice with unshakable grace. Eleanor Roosevelt transformed the role of First Lady into a platform for global human rights. Even back in the earliest days of American democracy, Abigail Adams reminded her husband John to "remember the ladies," with a clarity and wit that echoed through generations.

Powerful men throughout time have often had women beside them who were their equals in intellect, vision, and resilience—and sometimes, more than their equals. And lately, I've found myself drawn to one of them in particular.

I was lying in my hostel bunk in Vienna, Austria, when my French roommate, Camille, introduced herself and asked what I'd been up to during my visit. I told her all about the museums I'd explored and the landmarks I'd seen. I talked about how completely captivated I was by the charm and grandeur of the city. She smiled and said she was fascinated by Austria's history, especially how it once stood as the heart of a powerful empire in the 19th century.

"Do you know much about Empress Sisi?" She asked, casually.

I blinked. "I've actually never heard of her."

It's moments like these that always make me a little self-conscious about my limited knowledge of world history—wishing I'd paid a bit more attention in school. Because every time I travel, I'm reminded just how much I love learning about the past, how much I crave context for the places I walk through.

"She was the Empress of Austria," Camille explained. "I went to the Sisi Museum today. Her story is fascinating. There's actually a German Netflix series called *The Empress* that's based on her life. I highly recommend it."

"Oh, lovely! I'll definitely check it out," I said.

I've learned to take the recommendations of fellow travelers seriously. There's a kind of magic in the things strangers feel moved to share with you. That night, curled up in my bunk with headphones on and a blanket pulled to my chin, I started watching *The Empress*. I had no idea it would lead me down a rabbit hole of one of the most compelling women I'd ever learn about.

Elisabeth Amalie Eugenie of Bavaria, known to the world as Empress Sisi, was born in December 1837 into the Bavarian House of Wittelsbach, in present-day Munich, Germany. Unlike the typical aristocratic upbringing of her era, Sisi's early life was defined by freedom and nature rather than formal courtly constraint. She spent her childhood riding horses, hiking through the Bavarian countryside, and reading poetry—far removed from the stiff rituals and social expectations of the royal courts. Her upbringing instilled in her a deep love of solitude and movement, which would later come into sharp conflict with the rigid expectations of her roles as empress.

In the summer of 1853, while visiting the spa town of Bad Ischl, the young Austrian Emperor Franz Joseph I, ruler of the vast Habsburg Empire, was introduced to then 15-year-old Sisi. He had originally been expected to propose to her elder sister, Helene. But from the moment he saw Sisi, he was utterly captivated by her beauty, youth, and quiet defiance. Just two days after their first meeting, he broke with expectation and asked for Elisabeth's hand in marriage.

Eight months later, Sisi left behind the comfort and freedom of Munich to begin a new life in Vienna. A life that would one day be marked by both political prominence and deep personal struggle.

As Empress of Austria and later Queen of Hungary, Sisi quickly became one of the most iconic—and enigmatic—women in European royal history. While she was often praised for her grace and beauty, she also wielded influence behind the scenes, particularly in shaping Austro-Hungarian diplomacy. Her role in the Austro-Hungarian Compromise of 1867, which created the Dual Monarchy of Austria-Hungary, helped ease rising tensions between Austria and Hungary. Her deep sympathy for the Hungarian people and close relationship with Hungarian Prime Minister Gyula Andrássy earned her widespread respect and adoration in Hungary—a rare feat for a Habsburg royal.

But her influence was not limited to politics. Sisi challenged the expectations of royal womanhood in nearly every way. She resisted the ceremonial obligations of court life, often retreating from Vienna for long periods to travel across Europe and beyond. She was fiercely independent, intellectual, and deeply invested in her physical and mental well-being long before such ideas were common or accepted for women of her status. Her obsession with exercise, diet, and personal appearance is now seen through a more complex lens; part rebellion, part control in a world where she had so little.

Even in her later years, Sisi remained an elusive and compelling figure. Her tragic assassination in 1898 by an Italian anarchist only added to the mythology surrounding her. She was a woman who, despite the crown, never stopped searching for a kind of freedom that the empire could never offer her.

More than a century after her death, Sisi remains a cultural icon across Europe—not just for her beauty, but for her contradictions. She was a royal who longed for anonymity, a woman bound by tradition who rebelled against it, and a reluctant empress who nonetheless helped shaped one of Europe's most powerful empires.

Learning about Sisi in Vienna felt like uncovering a hidden thread of womanhood—one I hadn't expected to find, but somehow mirrored questions I carry with me. Her story wasn't just about monarchy or empire; it was about the tension so many women still feel today between who the world asks us to be and who we know ourselves to be.

I thought about how much pressure there still is, even now, to perform strength in certain ways. To be poised but not too loud. Elegant but not too soft. Powerful but not too much. And I thought about how Sisi refused to contort herself to fit these expectations. She was powerful in her own right, not because she mimicked male rulers, but because she embodied something else entirely: a strength rooted in vulnerability, in intuition, in tenderness, and in the audacity to live on her own terms.

As I continued exploring Vienna, and later Budapest, I carried Sisi's story with me. I wandered through grand palaces-turned-museums, stood beneath gilded ceilings and ornate chandeliers, and marveled at the Roman-inspired facades lining the streets. It was hard to fathom that people not so different from us with fears and hopes and longings just like ours once lived and ruled within those same walls.

There's something uncanny about standing in the remnants of empire. About knowing that centuries have passed, yet so much of who we are hasn't changed. We've advanced in technology and medicine. We've redefined borders, launched satellites into space, and hold the internet in the palm of our hands. And yet…our core humanity remains. We still ache for love. We still struggle to be understood. We still battle the same insecurities, longings, and power dynamics that shaped empires long ago.

That paradox of being both wildly evolved and stubbornly the same sits with me every time I travel. Why does it all feel so foreign, and yet so familiar?

Since returning from Vienna and Budapest, I've found myself in conversations with friends, with strangers, and even with myself about the ways gender continues to shape how we move through the world. About how men and women are so often positioned as opposites, as adversaries, rather than companions in the same human story. We coexist as one species, and yet biology, culture, and centuries of political power struggles have built walls between us. Walls we keep reinforcing, even when we claim to want connection.

And that's why, it's always been difficult for me to fully relate to the rhetoric—sometimes casual, sometimes cutting—that paints all men as broken, cruel, or irredeemable. I understand where it comes from; I've seen the harm caused by patriarchy; I've witnessed the pain inflicted by individual men in positions of power. But I've also been fortunate enough to have grown up surrounded by men who were kind, vulnerable, nurturing, and full of depth.

A week before my 25th birthday, I got one of those Snapchat memories—the kind that arrives uninvited and tugs at something tender. It was a selfie of me lying in the sun, taken exactly three years earlier. The caption read: "Last week being 21, feeling very bittersweet. Ready for what twenty-two has in store."

I looked at that younger version of myself and saw something familiar in my eyes: a mix of weariness and hope. Twenty-one had been a brutal year. My older brother, Christian, had fallen into a coma. I'd gone through a heart-wrenching breakup. And six months later, we lost MK. That season of life had gutted me in quiet, irreversible ways. Of course I was ready for the next chapter.

But what 21-year-old me didn't yet understand was that every chapter that follows—twenty-two, twenty-three, twenty-four—

would come with its own storms. I thought I'd already turned a page. But I was only just learning that life doesn't hand you a clean slate after hardship. It hands you a pen and asks you to keep writing anyway.

And no one modeled how to keep writing—how to keep going, even when the story takes an unexpected turn—more powerfully than my dad.

Just weeks after my 22nd birthday, my dad sat my siblings and me down and told us something that would change the course of all our lives. It was a truth he and my mom had been discreetly carrying for over a year, and one that required immense courage, vulnerability, and deep commitment to the integrity that had always defined him.

He was sitting on the living room couch when he called Christian and me over. There was something different in his voice— strained, uncertain. It was the first time I had ever seen my dad in a state that felt truly vulnerable, and I knew something was seriously wrong.

Christian and I walked over, side-eyeing each other with a kind of nervous grin—not out of amusement, but discomfort. We had no idea what we were walking into, and our bodies didn't quite know how to respond.

We sat down on either side of him. He kept his gaze fixed on the floor. This was something he never did. My dad, the man who always spoke with steadiness and eye contact, couldn't meet our eyes.

He began slowly, his voice cracking as he apologized. He said how sorry he was. How he never wanted to let us down. How he and my mom had done everything in their power to protect us— to protect our family.

Christian and I exchanged a look. The nervousness was gone now. This was serious.

"Whatever it is, Dad, you can tell us," Christian said gently, his voice steady as he tried to anchor the moment.

My dad's hands were trembling. When he finally spoke again, his words came out measured by heavy.

"There was an incident at work," he said. "A fellow employee accused me of sexual misconduct. And now… I'm being asked to step down from my position as a judge without pay. At least for the time being."

My heart sunk as I listened to my dad, now crying, go into details about the incident.

In just the last few years, my parents have opened up to my siblings and me about an alternative "lifestyle" they partake in. It's a choice that, for them, has been rooted in honesty, trust, and a desire to live authentically within their marriage.

Often referred to by outsiders as "swinging," the term barely scratches the surface of what this lifestyle truly represents. At its core, the alternative lifestyle is a relationship model outside of traditional monogamy—one that welcomes consensual, ethical non-monogamy in various forms. For some, that might look like open relationships or polyamory. For others, like my parents, it's a deeply personal agreement between two committed people to explore intimacy and connection with others, while remaining grounded in mutual respect, communication, and transparency.

And a common, subtle way that members of the lifestyle identify themselves is by wearing a ring on the opposite hand—the non-marital ring finger. It's not an overt announcement, just a symbol, one that others familiar with the community might recognize.

The woman who later accused my dad of misconduct had asked him about the ring.

He told her the truth.

He explained, perhaps more candidly than he should have in that moment, the lifestyle that he and my mom had chosen. He didn't brag. He didn't flirt. He wasn't inviting anything. But he crossed a line. He exercised poor judgement in a professional setting—one where boundaries, especially around power and consent, are crucial.

My dad has never denied that mistake. He didn't deflect or minimize it. He fully acknowledged that what he shared was inappropriate for the workplace. And while no physical misconduct occurred, and no proposition was made, the fact remained: his words were shared with someone in a subordinate role. That alone was enough to warrant disciplinary action. And it was enough to cost him the seat that he had held with integrity for years.

As he told Christian and me all of this, tears streamed down his face. I had never seen him like that—raw, vulnerable, exposed. He didn't hide behind his title. He didn't rewrite the story to protect his image. He faced us, his children, with nothing but the truth.

Between sobs, he kept repeating the same words over and over again. They were words that stayed with me ever since: "I just can't lose you guys and mom. I wouldn't know what to do without you."

It struck me, not just as the plea of a man in pain, but as the honest cry of someone who knew his strength had always been tethered to his family. He wasn't trying to escape the consequences. He was reckoning with the reality that love—true, grounded, equal love—was what he stood to lose most.

And as painful as it was to witness, it was also one of the most humanizing experiences of my life.

I didn't see him any differently. But I did see him more fully.

Because isn't that what we all want, deep down? To be seen not just in our triumphs, but in our failures. To be loved not despite our flaws, but through them. That day, my dad showed me that strength doesn't always look like stoicism or perfection.

Sometimes it looks like telling the truth even when it costs you. Sometimes it's crying in front of your children and trusting they'll still see you as whole.

But if I'm being honest, I was angry, too.

Angry that the world didn't get to see the version of my dad I knew: a man of compassion, of honesty, of love. Angry that the nuance of the situation was lost in headlines and soundbites. Angry that someone who had spent his entire career standing up for victims, listening to survivors, and holding abusers accountable, was now being painted as a creep—as someone to fear. It didn't match the man who had raised me. The man who drove my friends and me to dance practice, who made big Italian Sunday dinners, who shows up for me and the rest of my family every single day.

But nuance doesn't make for good news stories.

The media spun a narrative that left little room for complexity, for context, or grace. And in the wake of it all, my family faced a public shaming that most people will never understand.

And it was happening at a time when the world was already on fire. Donald Trump had finished his first term as President only two years before. The #MeToo movement had exploded—and rightly so. Brave women were coming forward with long-buried stories of sexual abuse, coercion, and violation. Stories that had been silenced, minimized, ignored. I believed those women. I *still* believe those women. I had women in my own life—friends, mentors, loved ones—who had survived the real and lasting traumas of sexual violence.

So how could I reconcile with all of this? It was a double-edged sword. One that cut through everything I thought I understood about fairness and truth. And while I still wrestle with the pain and confusion of that time, I also return to what I know: my father did not deserve to be vilified. He made a mistake. But he also told the truth when it would've been easier to lie not just to the court, or to the press, but to us. His family.

And that, to me, is integrity.

Since then, so much in our family has shifted. I haven't shared this story widely—only with those closest to me who know my dad and my mom, and who understand them beyond headlines and hearsay.

When my dad was asked to step down from his position, without pay, my mom stepped forward. She picked up the weight he had carried for years and held it without bitterness. She took on financial responsibilities, began working more hours, and poured herself into her career not just to survive, but to lead. It's strange how something so destabilizing became a catalyst for transformation.

She stepped up not just as a partner, but as a force. As our family's provider—though I've always hated that word, "breadwinner," like there's only room for one. The truth is, they became partners in a new way. And we, their children, got to witness what resilience and redefinition look like in real time.

As I've slowly started opening up about what happened, I've learned that our family's story isn't unique. A number of my friends have shared stories about their parents; about couples who had to switch roles, shift gears, and figure out new dynamics in response to life's curveballs, whether because of medical crises, financial upheaval, or personal reckoning.

I remember talking about it with my friend Kat during a visit to London. I was crashing at her place, sleeping on the air mattress she'd inflated in the middle of her one-bedroom flat. We'd spent the day wandering the city, and now we were flopped on our phones, half-scrolling, half-talking.

"Have I ever told you about the stuff that went down with my family a few years ago?" I asked, pausing mid-scroll.

"No, I don't think so. What happened?" She replied, looking up.

So, I told her. I walked her through it all—the confusion, the media, the way my dad sat us down and told the truth, the way my mom had to step forward. Kat listened the way she always does without interruption, and just enough nods and hums to let me know I was being heard.

"It's just been so crazy," I said. "Watching my dad have to let go of this role he held for so long—the provider, the protector. Seeing him carry this shame, this weight of vulnerability…it's been hard."

"Yeah, dude," Kat said softly. "I remember after my dad had his accident, he had such a hard time reconciling with that, too."

Kat's dad had worked as an elevator technician his whole life. He was the kind of man who fixed things—methodical, steady, proud of what his hands could do. Then, while Kat was still in high school, a steel rod fell on him while he was on the job, breaking his neck. He survived, but the accident forced him into early retirement long before he was ready, or willing.

"He ended up going into a deep depression," Kat said. "It was like… so much of what defined who he was had just been taken from him overnight. He just didn't know what to do with himself anymore. And it broke him in every way."

There was a strange kind of comfort that settled between us in that moment—not in our fathers' pain, but in the sharing of it. Two completely different families. Different careers, different circumstances. But the same sudden unraveling of identity.

Men who had built their sense of purpose on stability, usefulness, and provision only to have those pillars pulled out from beneath them. And in the wake of it all, what remained wasn't just fear or grief, but a deeper kind of loss: the loss of how they'd always seen themselves, and how they believed the world saw them too.

As daughters, we felt it. Not just as witnesses, but as part of the fallout. Watching the strongest men in our lives carry invisible wounds, unsure how to talk about them, unsure if they were even allowed to.

Kat and I talked for a long time that night about the unspoken rules that govern men's lives. About how vulnerability is something boys are taught to suppress, how strength is still so often equated with stoicism, financial dominance, and silence. About how those messages are passed down not always by words, but by example, by expectation, by cultural osmosis. And how the strongest men we've known, our fathers included, have had to unlearn those scripts in real time, often through pain and loss.

I thought back to my dad and how hard it was for him to step back. How vulnerable he looked on the couch that day he told us everything. And how much of his pain, I realized, came not just from what happened, but from what it meant for his role in our family. What it meant for how he saw himself as a man.

It made me think about how we tend to talk about gender roles in this binary, combative way: women reclaiming power from men, men stepping back to make room. But it's not war. Or at least, it shouldn't be. It's a reckoning. A reshaping. And that reshaping demands something from all of us. It demands compassion, conversation, and a redefinition of strength itself.

I've seen powerful men softened by even more powerful love. Not love that shrinks to fit beside them. But love that stands tall. Love that meets them where they are and dares them to grow.

My mom and dad. My brothers and their partners. My friends' fathers, like Kat's who've had to reinvent themselves after loss or injury or shame. I've seen how true partnership—like the kind I imagined between Franz Joseph and Sisi, even if only in moments has the capacity to reshape not just homes, but entire legacies.

Because the truth is, strength has never looked one way. And power, real power, has never been about domination or bravado. It's about truth. About being willing to say, "I'm scared" or "I need help" or "I don't know how to keep going, but I'm trying."

That's what my father showed me when he told us the truth.

That's what I look for in the people I love: not perfection, not performative strength, but softness. Humility. Willingness.

Sisi didn't rule with an iron fist. She didn't storm her way through palace halls demanding obedience. And yet, she shaped an empire. Her influence was real. Her gentleness was power. Her rebellion was quiet, but unwavering.

I think about how many women, across time and culture, have done the same. And how many men, if given permission, might feel safe enough to follow that model too.

Maybe that's why I bristle when I hear people say "men are trash" or adopt the "man-hater" identity as a defense mechanism. I get the impulse. The world has given us plenty of reasons to be wary, to armor up. But I also believe deeply that we cannot heal the harms of patriarchy by hardening ourselves against half the population.

We need softness. We need play. We need men who can cry, and women who can lead. We need fathers who apologize, and daughters who forgive. We need friendships and marriages and empires built on equality—not performative, box-checking equality—but the kind that roots itself in mutual reverence. That says: your strength doesn't scare me. It invites me to rise. And vulnerability *is* sexy.

That's what I'm learning.

From Sisi. From Kat. From my parents. From the way the sunlight filtered through the palaces of Vienna, centuries after her voice echoed through them. From the way the past reaches forward and offers us a choice.

We can keep living in separation.

Or we can build something truer.

Together.

Love Letters from a 20-Something

Chapter 12: Trips Around the Sun

Dear Reader,

Birthdays are magic.

Not just because of the confetti, the cake, or the carefully chosen cards, but the truth underneath it all: you're still here. Somehow, in a world that moves too fast and hurts too often, your heart kept beating. Your lungs kept rising and falling. You lived.

Another trip around the sun. Another 365 chances to be opened by joy and stitched back together by time. And whether you marked your birthday with a wild night out or a quiet night in, whether you were surrounded by friends or sitting alone with a cupcake and a candle—the point is, you made it. And that's worth honoring.

I think birthdays matter more than we let on. We outgrow the glittery hats and plastic crowns, we trade presents for text messages, and sometimes we forget that just being alive is worth celebrating. But I believe birthdays are sacred. They remind us that life isn't guaranteed. That every year we're given is a gift—and a choice.

Let's honor ourselves by hoping, healing, laughing, dancing. Keep showing up. And keep becoming the version of yourself you're meant to be.

This chapter celebrates the miracle of life and all of the small, ordinary, and extraordinary ways we live our lives.

Keep living and keep loving.

✱✱✱

The idea of a birthday has been around a lot longer than balloons and sheet cake. The very first mentions come from Ancient Egypt, where birthdays weren't about aging another year but about transformation. When a Pharaoh was crowned, it was seen as the day he was "born" as a god. These coronation celebrations, dating back as far as 3,000 BCE, marked the Pharaoh's divine beginning. The Hebrew Bible even references one such celebration for an Egyptian ruler.

As with so many traditions, the Greeks borrowed the idea and made it their own. To honor the gods, they baked moon-shaped cakes for Artemis, goddess of the moon. To capture her radiance, they topped the cakes with lit candles, so they glowed like the night sky. Sound familiar? That's where the ritual of cake and candles is thought to have begun.

Ironically, despite being home to the most celebrated birthday in the world, Christmas, the early Christian church considered birthdays pagan and evil. For the first few centuries, no candles, no cakes, no parties. That changed in the fourth century, when the birth of Jesus began to be celebrated, partly to attract those already observing Saturnalia, a rowdy Roman holiday.

The Romans, meanwhile, were the first to throw birthday parties for ordinary (well, ordinary male) citizens. Women weren't included until around the 12th century. They even declared public holidays for birthdays of prominent leaders, setting the stage for the culture of grand celebrations and gift-giving.

Fast-forward to 18th-century Germany, where birthdays began to look more like what we know today. Kinderfeste, or children's birthday celebrations, featured cakes with candles to mark each year of life, plus one extra candle symbolizing hope for the year ahead. The tradition of blowing them out and making a wish? That started there, too.

From Pharaohs to peasants, gods to Kinderfeste, birthdays have always been about more than marking time. They're about meaning. They remind us of who we are, who we belong to, and the miracle of having been born at all. Maybe that's why I've always felt birthdays so deeply. Not just as dates on a calendar, but as little altars to meaning.

That sense of meaning has always been true for me. If you know me, you know I take my birthday very seriously. It falls right in the middle of July—a personal halfway mark through the year—

and when people ask what my favorite holiday is, I usually say, "my birthday." I laugh when I say it, but I'm only half joking. The truth is, I've been making a big deal out of my birthday for as long as I can remember. Ever since I was a little girl, it's been a day I've claimed fully—a celebration of life, joy, and the simple, beautiful fact of being here another year.

But as much as I love my birthday, I know not everyone greets another year of life with the same enthusiasm. I've seen countless trending videos, and had more than a few heartfelt conversations with friends, about people crying on their birthday. For some, the recognition of their journey, their achievements, and the person they've become doesn't spark celebration. Instead, it can stir up an internal weight of expectations, an inner voice insisting they haven't done enough. And for others, the sadness comes from past disappointments—moments when they felt overlooked, or when the people they hoped would show up simply didn't, leaving them with the sting of feeling forgotten.

I can empathize with those who maybe just see their birthday as another day. But what I have learned over the years is this: you have to treat your birthday the way you want your day to be treated. Just as the saying goes, *treat others as you wish to be treated,* the same applies to yourself. Celebrate the way you wish to be celebrated. And the people who have taught me this most are my friends—the ones who've shown up year after year, who've reminded me that celebration is as much about who's beside you as it is about the candles on the cake.

My best friend, Lindsey, has celebrated more birthdays with me than not. Friends since we were two years old, she has been in my life longer than my younger siblings have. Together, we've grown up side by side. From preschoolers to little ballerinas in toe shoes, to cringe-worthy middle schoolers flashing peace signs in our iPad selfies. Now, we're two women and best friends who have seen more of the world than we ever dreamed possible as children.

On a snowy February night, we celebrated Lindsey's 23rd birthday with pre-drinks before heading out to the Disco. I remember how beautiful she looked. She was happy, glowing, her smile wide as she soaked in the love of the people around her.

With a few drinks warming me, I went up to her and said, "Happy Birthday, Lu. I hope you know how much you deserve to be celebrated today and every day. You're always the one celebrating others, but I need you to feel how deeply loved you are. I don't think you hear it enough, and I want you to believe it."

Lindsey's birthday falls on the very first day of Pisces. And like so many Pisces I've known, she embodies that same unmistakable energy—caring, selfless, and endlessly understanding. Add to that her long, curly blonde hair and graceful ballerina legs, and she could easily be mistaken for a Disney princess come to life.

She carries a gentle charisma, soulful and understated, always putting others first and approaching life as a creative problem-solver to her core. We grew up as dancers together performing in the *Nutcracker* each year and choreographing our own routines to songs we can still remember by heart. On stage, we were often cast in the same role, alternating performances. Our movements mirrored each other so naturally that even our choreographers would pair us, knowing we shared the same rhythm and flow.

We were two peas in a pod for the first decade of our lives, and as we grew older, we naturally grew into two very different people—yet always tethered by the same lust for life. Lindsey's journeys took her deep into nature, hiking through the Swiss Alps and road-tripping across the U.S., while mine carried me through the streets of the world's great cities, walking for hours just to feel their pulse.

We share the same curiosity, the same hunger to explore, but our expressions of it look different. Her through mountains and trails, me through skylines and winding boulevards. And in that contrast, we've found not distance, but balance—two parallel paths that will always loop back to each other.

We see the world through a similar lens, and even in the differences that make us our own unique selves, there's a shared love and appreciation for life. It's one that feels like the greatest gift you could hope for in a best friend of more than two decades.

But the same qualities that make Lindsey so selfless and caring can also become her heaviest burden. She has a way of putting others first without hesitation, and without question, sometimes to the point of forgetting her own needs. And because she pours so much of herself into others, there are moments when she's left feeling drained or unseen, as if all that giving has gone unnoticed. That balance, over time, can plant doubt, reinforcing the belief that she isn't enough.

The truth is that's often the paradox of people like Lindsey—people who love with their whole hearts. Their light is so steady, so reliable, that others forget to tell them how brightly they shine. They become the stronghold, the comfort, the one everyone turns to, and yet they rarely hear those same words of reassurance in return.

But Lindsey is more than enough. She always has been. And if you're lucky enough to have a friend like her, you learn that reminding them of their worth isn't just kind, it's essential. Birthdays, especially, become not only a celebration of another year, but a chance to turn all that love back toward them. And that's why I've always leaned fully into my own birthdays, too. If I want the people I love to feel seen, I've had to let myself be celebrated in the same way.

I think back to my 25th birthday in Las Vegas, celebrated with five of my closest friends. My grandma had given me a pink "Birthday Girl" sash, and I wore it everywhere through the hotel, at the pool, in the clubs. For three days it hardly came off.

By hour twelve, we found ourselves at a day club, surrounded by music, sunlight and thick desert heat—105 degrees at least. I walked up to the bar in my black bikini and birthday sash, ordering a frozen margarita to cool off. While waiting, I struck up a conversation with a group of cousins from Minnesota. The bar was crowded, loud, full of summertime energy. Then, through the blur of voices and bodies, a man passed behind me, locked eyes with mine, and shouted: *"Happy birthday! Live a long life."*

I haven't been able to let go of those four words since. It wasn't just a passing birthday wish. It had felt more like a benediction, a call to attention. The way he said it—direct, intentional, looking me straight in the eyes—landed in me like both blessing and challenge. His words stayed with me long after the music faded, echoing as a question: what does it actually mean to live a long life?

For me, the answer is clear—I only have to look at my mom. Aging has only ever made her shine brighter. She raised five kids while working full-time, somehow making it all look effortless, and for more than a decade she's built and run her own therapeutic practice. She has never let her identity collapse into being *just* a mom or a wife—though she has been extraordinary at both. She has always carved out space for herself, proving that presence for others is strongest when you also show up for yourself.

Even now, with all five of us grown, she continues to invest in her own life. She goes to pilates multiple times a week, keeps her hair freshly done, wears the cutest and most trendy clothes, and carries herself with a confidence that feels timeless. She still shows up for us kids, and for my dad, but most importantly, she shows up for herself.

To me, that is what it means to live a long life: putting in effort not because something is wrong, but because something still matters. My mom reminds me every day that life doesn't end when your children leave the house, when your career becomes routine, or when the world might expect you to fade quietly into the background. She chooses instead to shine. She is proof that living fully is not about clinging to youth, but about embracing every season as if it's still worth dressing up for, still worth loving yourself for.

I feel like the luckiest girl in the world to have a role model like that to look up to. My mom shows me every day that aging doesn't have to mean shrinking, that each year can actually be an expansion into new joys, new routines, and new ways of loving yourself.

As I watch her age, I don't fear what the next years will bring. I see her pilates classes, her fresh hair blowouts, her cute clothes, and I realize that getting older doesn't mean dimming your life— it means choosing to keep it lit. Instead of resisting the years, she embraces them, finding ways to shine a little brighter with each one.

That example has freed me from some of the expectations I used to carry. As a woman, my role in life is not just to be a mother or a wife. Those identities are beautiful, but they aren't the sum of who I am or who I will be. Watching my mom reminds me that identity isn't a box to step into once and for all. Instead, it's something we continue to write and rewrite as long as we're alive.

My mom has always said that she has never cared about what us kids end up doing for a living, who or if we marry, or whether we choose to have kids of our own. What she cares about is simple: that we are, in her words, "good and happy people in this world."

Those values—goodness, happiness—have become my compass. It strips away the noise of comparison, the pressure of timelines, the weight of measuring life by milestones. It reminds me that another year isn't about checking boxes, but about asking: *Am I a good person? Am I happy? Am I living in a way that reflects both?*

And maybe that's the true magic of birthdays. They aren't just celebrations of age; they're invitations to pause and take stock. To look at the year behind us with honesty and the year ahead with hope. To ask whether the life we're living is one that feels meaningful, and if not, to give ourselves permission to rewrite it.

It's a truth I've found echoed outside my family too, in the words I've come back to again and again. My friend Matthew has a plaque in his room that I've read so many times, I practically have it memorized. It reads:

"We will remember… all our lives. And even if we are occupied with important things, even if we attain honor or fall into misfortune… still let us remember how good it once was here, when we were all together…united by a good and kind feeling, which made us, for the first time…better perhaps than we are."—Fyodor Dostoevsky

These words get me every time. The idea that in some passing moments, simply by being together, we become something better. That goodness, that unity, is what stays. Not the accomplishments or the failures, not the titles or the years, but the memory of having once belonged to something kind. Dostoevsky seems to suggest that this is what lasts. That when we look back across the sweep of our lives, it won't be the milestones that define us so much as the moments we were truly present with one another.

And isn't that, in its own way, the essence of living a long life? Not just surviving the years but filling them with moments that make us "better perhaps than we are." Birthdays remind me of this. They aren't just about marking time; they are invitations to pause, to gather, to notice the good that's already here. To remember who we've been, and to bless who we're becoming.

Birthdays ask us to notice the sacred in the ordinary: the laughter around a crowded table, the glow of candles in a dark room, the voices rising in imperfect harmony. For a moment, life slows down. For a moment, we are reminded that presence itself is a gift—that being here, together, is enough.

And maybe that's the truest wish we make when we blow out the candles: not for more years, but for more moments like these. Moments that make us better, kinder, more alive. Moments that remind us that another trip around the sun is never just about survival. It's about connection, about joy, about remembering how good it is, right now, to be here.

From Pharaohs to Kinderfeste, from coronations to candles, birthdays have always carried the same heartbeat: a reminder that life is worth noticing. My own birthdays—Vegas heat, Lindsey's laughter, my mom's resilience—are just modern echoes of an ancient truth. The details change, but the meaning stays: to celebrate another year is to say, we are still here.

So, when your next birthday comes, don't wait for someone else to make it meaningful. Claim it. Celebrate in the way that feels true to you—alone with coffee and reflection, or loudly with music and friends, or somewhere in between. Let it be a moment to pause, to gather, to remember who you've been and to bless who you're becoming. After all, another trip around the sun is never guaranteed. That's what makes it worth celebrating.

Because birthdays aren't just about getting older. They're about getting closer—closer to ourselves, to each other, to the truth that being alive is the greatest gift of all. Another year, another candle, another chance to live a long life by making it count.

Chapter 13: There's a Reason Why It's a Journey

Dear Reader,

Mental health is one of those things we all think we understand until life reminds us that knowing about it is not the same as living it. We've made progress in how we talk about it, sure. We have words now that didn't exist generations ago. We have research, diagnoses, therapies, medications. We say, "it's okay not to be okay." And yet, for so many of us, mental health is still something we whisper about. Something that carries weight and stigma. Something that feels lonely, even in a crowded room.

I grew up surrounded by conversations about wellness. I learned the language of self-care, of trauma, of healing. I believed in it wholeheartedly. But it wasn't until my own world cracked—until depression and later anxiety found me—that mental health stopped being an abstract idea and became something I carried in my own chest.

This chapter is about that journey—not the tidy, polished version where everything gets better overnight, but the messy, human one. The one where you fall apart and put yourself back together, sometimes a hundred times over. The one where asking for help feels like the bravest thing you've ever done. The one where you learn that mental illness doesn't make you broken, and healing doesn't make you weak—it makes you alive.

If you're struggling, I hope these words remind you that you're not alone. If you love someone who's struggling, I hope they help you hold space for their story with gentleness and grace. Because mental health is not a straight path, and it's not a solitary one either. It's a journey—and it's one we're all still learning how to walk.

✳✳✳

I've always been educated about mental health. It was part of my upbringing, my schooling, my understanding of how people move through the world. I grew up knowing the language of wellness—how trauma shapes us, how emotions live in the body, how therapy can be a lifeline. I studied it. I believed in it. I knew how important it was.

And for a long time, I thought that knowing about mental health meant I understood it. But there's a vast difference between understanding mental illness as a concept and living with it in your own skin. That part didn't come for me until I was sixteen after a traumatic car accident that left me shaken in ways no textbook could prepare me for.

We've come a long way in how we talk about mental health. But the truth is, it's still not enough. Not long ago, the field was less about healing and more about hiding. In the 18th and 19th centuries, "madness" was locked away in asylums. People suffering from depression, anxiety, trauma, or psychosis were seen as problems to be contained, not humans to be understood. Treatments ranged from crude isolation to horrific "cures" that stripped people of dignity and autonomy.

By the early 1900s, figures like Freud began shifting the conversation, introducing ideas about the unconscious, talk therapy, and the connection between mind and behavior. But mental illness remained stigmatized as a mark of deviance, weakness, or moral failing.

Fast forward a century, and we've gained language, research, and resources. We understand brain chemistry, trauma, and social factors in ways that were unimaginable before. We've built therapies, medications, campaigns telling us it's "okay not to be okay." And yet, stigma persists. People still hesitate to ask for a mental health day. We're told to "just think positive," as if our minds are machines that can be reset at will. Entire systems treat symptoms but fail to nurture healing.

I think that's why my first experience with depression felt so destabilizing. Because despite everything I knew, and everything I'd been taught, I still didn't know what to do when it was me.

It was my junior year of high school, on what should have been an ordinary Thursday morning. I was a newly licensed driver, gripping the steering wheel, making the same turns I made every day on the way to school.

Halfway through my route, I eased into a left turn, the light green in my favor, when out of nowhere a car tore through the intersection. A man blew past the red light and slammed into me, the impact hitting in a single second. The airbags deployed at my side, leaving the acrid smell of gunpowder in the air and a ringing in my ears. My chest tightened, my hands trembling against the wheel as the shock sank in.

I fumbled for my phone, dialing my dad with shaking fingers. When he answered, my voice cracked with words barely forming between sobs and short, panicked breaths. "Daddy...I—I just got hit," I stammered, my chest heaving.

Around me, traffic kept moving. Car horns blared, strangers yelling at me to move, as if I were just another inconvenience in their commute. They couldn't see what had just happened. They couldn't see that the other driver had sped off, leaving me stranded and stunned in the middle of the wreckage.

"Okay, okay!" I yelled out of instinct, though no one could hear me, tears streaming hot down my face. My whole body was shaking, adrenaline roaring in my ears. Somehow, I managed to pull my smashed car over to the side of the road, my breath shallow and uneven.

That moment—that helplessness, and that sudden reminder of how fragile everything is—never left me. It carved out a permanent space in my memory. It was the first truly traumatic event of my life, and it changed how I understood mental health. Not as something abstract or clinical, not just words in a textbook or lessons in a classroom, but as a visceral, lived experience.

In the weeks that followed, the fear followed me like a shadow. I couldn't get behind the wheel. Even as a passenger, my body would tense at every intersection, every flash of brake lights, every oncoming car. Some mornings before school, I'd sit on my bed frozen, tears streaming, unable to convince my body it was safe. My mind replayed the accident on a loop, and eventually that fear bled into sadness, into exhaustion, into my first real depression.

And yet, I don't think what I went through was unique. Most teenagers experience their first storms of mental health struggles during those years. It's biology as much as circumstance. Our brains are still under construction in adolescence. The emotional centers are fully fired up while the parts responsible for logic, regulation, and perspective are still wiring themselves together. Everything feels more intense because, in a way, it is. Joy is electric, heartbreak is unbearable, fear hits like a tidal wave. Even without trauma, teenage years are a time when sadness, moodiness, and anxiety can ebb and flow.

We write off our teenage mood swings as drama or hormones. So, it's no wonder those years feel like the end of the world sometimes. Your brain is literally trying to make sense of a universe it hasn't yet built the tools to navigate. Everything feels sharp, urgent, monumental. But on the flip side of that intensity is how fiercely resilient the teenage brain can be.

I was lucky. I had support around me—friends, family, teachers who showed up without judgment—and slowly, my world began to feel safe again. The accident had shaken something in me, a sense of security I hadn't even realized I was carrying until it was gone. But eventually, everything started to feel more manageable. Life moved forward, and I was eager to throw myself into the next big moments that waited for me.

By the time high school ended and college began, the heavy fog of depression that had followed the accident had mostly lifted, retreating to the occasional, familiar weight of seasonal depression. It's something a lot of us experience. The subtle shift in mood when the seasons change, when the daylight slips away earlier, and the world feels a little darker and colder. Scientists link it to our circadian rhythms, to the way our brains respond to shorter days and less sunlight.

It's not the same as those deep, consuming depressions, but it still demands something of us. It tells us to keep reaching for warmth and light when the world outside feels unbearably dim.

As I moved through college, I found myself immersed in social work classes where "self-care" was treated like gospel. Professors reminded us over and over that you cannot pour from an empty cup, that this line of work would ask more of us than we could ever imagine. They gave us how-to guides on self-care, handed out journal prompts that urged us to list the things we were doing, or supposed to be doing, to protect our mental health. It was part of our training, preparing us for a profession notorious for its imbalance: overworked and underpaid, often caught in the cycle of compassion fatigue while carrying the weight of other people's stories, traumas, and needs.

Once I began my fieldwork, everything I had read in textbooks and underlined in lecture notes suddenly came alive in a much more human way. I was no longer just studying theories about trauma, mental illness, and systemic injustice; I was walking into people's lives and seeing it up close. And it wasn't just me. My classmates would return from their placements carrying stories that weighed on their shoulders, each of us trying to process the rawness of what we were witnessing.

We'd gather in classrooms or coffee shops and swap experiences, talking about families struggling to survive, the kids who didn't have the tools to regulate their emotions, the immigrants who sought out services while seeking asylum from war in their home countries. We spoke in low voices about the anxieties we were carrying home with us, how impossible it sometimes felt to leave the work at the door.

And while I nodded along, understanding the words they used, I didn't fully understand the feeling. I empathized, of course. I saw the same things they did. But anxiety was still an abstract concept to me. Anxiety was something I knew how to define, how to support in others, but had never felt in my own body. I didn't yet know what it was like to wake up with your chest already tight, or to feel a thought spiral out of your control. At that point in my life, anxiety still belonged to other people's stories.

Anxiety and depressive disorders are the two most common mental health diagnoses in the Western world. They're often referred to as the "common cold" of mental health. Not because they're mild or easy to manage, but because they're everywhere. They cross borders and demographics, touching people of every age, gender, and background. Millions of us live with them each year often unseen.

For a long time, I only knew one side of that statistic. I had walked through depression before, felt its heaviness pull me under, but I had never fully understood what it meant to live with anxiety. Not until recently when it slipped into my life uninvited.

It started creeping in slowly after I was robbed at knifepoint while living in London. I've always had a deep connection between my mind and body; they've always spoken to each other, telling me when something was wrong, keeping me level. People have often told me I carry a calming presence, that my demeanor feels like an anchor that grounds them.

But after that night, the anchor slipped. The calmness that had felt like the core of who I was—something steady, reliable, almost instinctive—began to unravel. My body stayed on high alert long after the danger had passed, like it didn't believe it was truly over. My heart raced at random moments; my chest tightened at the smallest unknowns. Sleep came in fractured pieces, and every street corner, every shadow, felt like it might hold a threat.

I told myself it was just the trauma talking, that it would fade with time. But instead, the anxiety grew louder. It wasn't just a whisper in the back of my mind anymore. It had settled into my body, rewiring me from the inside out. My nervous system had decided the world wasn't safe, and it wouldn't let me forget it.

So, when I finally boarded the plane back to Denver, I thought coming home might reset something in me. I thought familiarity would soothe the jagged edges of my fear. But the truth is, I was returning a different person—a version of myself I hadn't met before. Fiercely independent. Sharper around the edges. Carrying memories and friendships that no one at home could fully understand. And carrying, too, the ache of having been truly lonely for the first time in my life.

You'd think that after all that—after a year of surviving on my own in a foreign country—I'd be able to handle anything that came next. But the moment I landed, it all hit me harder than I expected.

I was moving back in with my parents after having tasted freedom for a year. My bank account was barely scraping above empty, and there was no new job waiting for me on the other side of customs. The plan I'd built up in my mind to save enough money to return to London by the start of the new year suddenly felt like sand slipping through my hands. Every thought spiraled into the next.

And layered on top of all that was the pressure of planning a trip to Vietnam with G for our brother, Christian's wedding. It was something that should've been nothing but joy, but instead felt like one more spinning plate I wasn't sure I could keep in the air. My chest stayed tight. My mind ran laps. There was no safe landing, not even at home.

Still, in the short months before Vietnam, I hustled. I picked up every odd job I could, scraping together just enough money to make the trip happen. G and I decided we'd make it count: at least two weeks abroad, giving the twenty-four-hour journey across oceans some justice, adding Northern Thailand to the itinerary like we always dreamed of doing together.

As the departure date drew closer, a flicker of genuine excitement broke through the static of my anxiety. I couldn't wait to see my brother, to meet his wife's family, to be part of their special day. And I couldn't wait to have that time with G—to fall back into the familiarity of our shared adventures and late-night talks with strangers in hostels.

And honestly, the journey there was everything I needed it to be. We survived the marathon flight, watched the sunrise spill across the Pacific from tiny plane windows, and stepped off the final flight to meet Christian and Meo Meo with anticipation. The first few days in Vietnam were magic as we walked through the streets of Ho Chi Minh City with its maze of motorbikes. I watched Christian move through his new home like he'd been there forever. It was beautiful to see him rooted in this other corner of the world, building a life that felt entirely his own.

I felt honored just to witness it all. To sit in tiny restaurants where the tables were crowded with dishes I couldn't pronounce. To hear the sounds of scooters and street vendors winding through alleyways, to breathe in a city alive with scents of fish sauce and jasmine. For a moment, it felt like maybe this trip would give me the reset I craved—a break from the anxiety that had been sitting in me for months.

But underneath the wonder of it all, there was a noise I couldn't turn off. A low, persistent voice in my head that followed me from one breathtaking scene to the next. No matter how beautiful the setting, my body stayed on edge, like it didn't trust the calm I was trying to offer it.

We left Ho Chi Minh City and booked a 24-hour whirlwind stop in Bangkok before heading to Chiang Mai. It was me, G, and Christian's best friend, Eric. None of us had a place to stay lined up, deciding instead to pull an all-nighter in a city that seemed to never sleep. We threw ourselves into it all—cheering at a brutal Muay Thai fight, eating food that burned our tongues and made us laugh, drinking rooftop cocktails as the city glimmered endlessly below us. Later, we danced shoulder to shoulder to live music with tourists and locals in a packed Irish pub. It was the perfect night.

By the time the mics were turned off and the last round was poured, it was nearly dawn. We slung our backpacks over our shoulders, still tipsy, still grinning, and headed straight for the airport. Our flight to Chiang Mai left at 5.a.m., promising a slower pace and days of adventure in Northern Thailand before returning to Vietnam for the wedding.

But by the time we landed in Chiang Mai and checked into our hostel, the fun and craziness of Bangkok felt far away. My body wasn't just tired, it was shutting down.

I wish I could say this was new. That after years of late nights in college and long weekends traveling, my immune system had toughened up. But it hasn't. It never has. Anytime I mix lack of sleep with too much drinking, my body calls it quits. And after a 24-hour bender in Bangkok, this was no exception.

At first, it felt like a standard hangover layered with the beginnings of a cold: a pounding head, a scratchy throat, the kind of fatigue that makes every step feel like a chore. But then came the bumps—tiny, itchy welts that started on my hands and crept up my arms, across my stomach, multiplying as the hours went on.

I tried everything from Benadryl to cold compresses, to deep breaths but nothing worked. And the longer they stayed, the more my anxiety flared. I told myself it was just an allergic reaction, something harmless. But deep down, I knew better. My body was sounding the alarm, mirroring the chaos in my head.

The connection between my mind and body—the one I usually trust to warn me when something's wrong and guide me back to calm—had completely unraveled. I felt hijacked by my own nervous system.

And all I wanted, desperately, was to enjoy where I was. To be present. To laugh with G and Eric, to take in every ounce of Thailand the way I had dreamed I would. But instead, I was shrinking inward. Some nights I'd peel away early, retreating to my hostel bunk long before anyone else was ready to call it a night. Other times, I'd stay out, but it was like my body was somewhere else. I was entirely unfocused, detached, like I was watching the trip happen through someone else's eyes.

That's the thing about anxiety. It has a way of stealing even the most beautiful moments. It takes the view, the laughter, the company and turns it into background noise to whatever else is happening in your own head.

The worst part was that I wasn't able to name any of it. I expressed how uncomfortable I felt in my body to G, how I just didn't "feel good". But what really came across more was me being irritable and on edge. I was not myself at all and I could tell it was hard for people to be around me.

After grabbing street food one night, the three of us—G, Eric, and I—decided to walk down the block for Thai massages.

"Hold on," I said abruptly, stopping in my tracks. My voice sounded strange, like it wasn't coming from me. "I feel... really weird. Like I'm about to pass out."

G turned immediately, concern flashing across her face. "Okay, let's sit for a second," she said, already steering me toward a low wall by the sidewalk. "Do you need water? Food? Anything?"

I sat down, my legs shaky, my hands clammy. "I don't know," I said, my words uneven. "Everything feels wrong. My whole body feels like it's on edge, like I'm not even here."

Eric crouched in front of me. "Want me to grab you some Benadryl? Just in case it's another reaction?"

"Yeah, maybe," I nodded, rubbing my hands together like I could wring the feeling out of them. "God, I just... I don't know what's happening. I feel like I'm coming out of my own skin."

"It's okay," G said, wrapping an arm around my shoulders. "I'll stay here with you until you're ready."

Eric headed back to our hostel, leaving just the two of us in the thick, humid night. And then it all came spilling out—all the things I'd been holding in for months. How since moving back home, I'd been living in a state of constant unease. How anxiety, this alien feeling I'd never known before London, had followed me across the ocean and taken up residence in my body. How foreign food and unfamiliar smells only amplified it, leaving me feeling exposed, fragile, disconnected from myself.

G just listened, her hand steady on my back. "I hear you," she said quietly. "You'll be okay, I promise. You're not alone."

And for a moment, sitting there on a foreign street corner under flickering neon lights, I felt the tiniest bit of relief. Not because the anxiety had left, but because someone else could finally see it, too.

That moment changed everything for me. It was the first time I admitted out loud that I wasn't okay. The first time I named the thing that had been silently eating away at me for months. And while naming it didn't make it disappear, it was my first step toward understanding what I was really dealing with.

I wish I could say that realization made the rest of the trip easier, but it didn't. Anxiety stayed with me through the temples and night markets, through plane rides and crowded streets. I wasn't just "feeling weird" or "off." I was living with anxiety. And that meant I could slowly begin to learn how to live with it instead of running from it. Coming home after that trip made one thing undeniable: I needed help. I told the people closest to me everything—how my body felt like it was betraying me, how I couldn't control the spirals in my head, how genuinely sick I was for so much of the trip.

I returned with a deeper empathy for the millions of people I'd studied and read about in classrooms and case studies. It made me see my own friends differently, those who live with anxiety or depression every single day. Mental illness stopped being an abstract "issue". It became human. It became real.

And I think about how lucky I was, for so long, not to know that reality firsthand. How blessed I was to move through most of my life without all those uncomfortable feelings in my body. But trauma doesn't care about timing. It doesn't care about how "strong" or "prepared" you are. It leaves marks—tiny, invisible prints on your brain and nervous system—that don't wash away just because you've crossed a border, found safety, or tried to convince yourself you're fine.

And maybe that's the most important thing I've learned about mental health: it isn't linear. It doesn't always make sense. And it doesn't make you weak. It just makes you human.

I decided I couldn't keep living at the mercy of my anxiety. I was tired of feeling hijacked by my own mind, of waiting for the next spiral to knock me down. So, I chose to take control—not in the sense of "fixing" myself overnight, but by finally reaching out for help.

I connected with a therapist and psychiatrist. I shared all the things I'd been carrying and started on a medication that could help level out the chaos in my brain. And in all honesty, starting medication was scary. There's a stigma around it, like taking something for your mind makes you weaker than someone who doesn't need it. But the truth is, it made me stronger. It gave me enough steadiness to start doing the deeper work of understanding myself.

The more I sat with my own experience, the more I realized how little room we're given to talk about mental health openly. Even now, in a world where "self-care" is a buzzword and therapy is "trendy", there's still a blanket of silence around real mental illness. We're praised for productivity but pitied for panic attacks.

We're told to "just relax", "just think positive," as if our minds are machines that can be reset with a single command.

And yet, anxiety and depression are everywhere. The "common cold" of mental health, they say. And instead of offering compassion, society hands us shame.

Before I experienced anxiety and depression for myself, I thought I understood. I thought empathy meant listening to my friends talk about their struggles, studying the diagnostic criteria in my undergraduate courses, reading articles about mental illness. But living it is different. Living it means knowing what it's like to feel unsafe inside your own skin; to have your thoughts loop so loud they drown everything else out, to lose yourself to fear you can't comprehend.

I don't think there's one "right" way to manage mental health. But I do know this: asking for help is not weakness. It's courage. And it makes a difference.

So, if you're struggling: please hear this: you are not broken. You're not "too much" or "not enough." What you're carrying is real, and you don't have to carry it alone. Reach out. Say the hard thing. Take the hand that's offered. Find the therapist, take the medication, lean on your people. Do whatever you need to do to keep going because your life is worth that effort.

And if you love someone who's fighting their own invisible battle, remember this: mental illness doesn't always look how you expect it to. It isn't weakness or laziness or a lack of willpower. It's heavy and complex, and it takes time to heal. Offer patience instead of platitudes. Sit with them in the hard moments instead of trying to fix them. Remind them they're not a burden. Because sometimes, the smallest act of love is enough to pull someone back from the edge.

There's a reason why it's called a journey. We don't get to choose whether mental illness exists in this world, but we do get to choose how we meet it: with silence and stigma, or with compassion and understanding.

And if there's one thing I hope we choose, every time, it's compassion. Because compassion saves lives. Sometimes, it even saves your own.

Chapter 14: The World Doesn't Care—And That's Liberating

Dear Reader,

There comes a point when you realize the world isn't watching as closely as you thought it was. That people are far more preoccupied with their own lives, their own insecurities, than they are with your choices, your mistakes, or your dreams. At first, that realization can sting—like maybe you don't matter as much as you hoped. But if you sit with it a little longer, it starts to feel like freedom.

Because if the world doesn't care, then you get to decide who you want to be. You get to show up fully, unapologetically, without waiting for permission or approval. That's where trust comes in. Not necessarily the kind we place in others, but the kind we learn to place in ourselves. The kind that says: You're allowed to be exactly who you are. And you don't owe anyone any explanation for it.

For so long, I lived at the mercy of imagined audiences and fear-soaked what-ifs. What if I fail? What if I change and no one understands? What if I take the leap and fall flat on my face? But somewhere along the way, I started asking different questions. What if I succeed? What if I feel proud? What if the person I become is even better than the one I left behind?

That shift from fear to possibility changed everything.

This chapter is about that shift. About what it means to live for yourself in a world that's constantly trying to shape you. About trading perfection for presence, and shame for sovereignty. It's a reminder that you don't need to be anyone other than who you already are, and there's no reason not to chase the life that makes you feel most alive.

Because the truth is: the world doesn't care. And maybe that's exactly why you should.

***

As a society, we tend to agree that trust is a cornerstone of any meaningful relationship. We want to believe that the people we live with, work with, and love will do everything they can not to hurt us. But how do we actually know if we can trust someone? Is it earned through consistent actions? Through time and patience?

The uncomfortable truth is you can't ever *truly* know. Not with absolute certainty. And perhaps more importantly, placing your trust solely in someone else and expecting them to hold it flawlessly is a fragile foundation.

Because trust, when rooted only in others, becomes a projection: a belief, a hope, an expectation that someone will act the way we need them to. But that also means we're handing over the responsibility for our emotional safety to someone outside of ourselves. And when that trust is broken, it can leave us feeling powerless, betrayed, or even victimized.

Worse, we can start to confuse trust with control by believing that if we trust someone, they're now obligated to protect our feelings, to never disappoint us, to be loyal in the ways we define. But trust isn't about guaranteeing outcomes. It's about choosing to live open-heartedly, knowing that you can handle what happens even if someone lets you down.

True security doesn't come from trusting others *never* to hurt us. It comes from trusting ourselves to recover, to respond, and to keep showing up as who we are, no matter what.

Just before I left for a month-long trip across Eastern Europe, I had started seeing someone named Joshua. It was new, exciting, and a little undefined—exactly the way some of the best things begin. We hadn't had the "what are we" conversation, and neither of us seemed in a rush to pin anything down. Still, as my departure date drew closer, a question tugged at me not out of jealousy, but curiosity. Maybe even care.

One evening, just days before I left, I asked him, playfully, "Soooo...you gonna be kissing any girls while I'm away?"

He smirked. "I don't know. *You're* the one jetting off to be around a bunch of Europeans."

"Mmm, okay. Fair enough," I laughed. "Well, I don't think that'll be a problem. I just hope you don't either."

And that was it. No tension. No unspoken expectation. Just an easy, honest exchange wrapped in mutual respect. There was something refreshing about how we both acknowledged the uncertainty without trying to control it.

While it was a simple conversation, it marked something significant for me. For the first time in a long time, I wasn't bracing for disappointment or reading between the lines. I wasn't trying to decode intentions or protect myself preemptively. I was just…present. And that felt like healing.

It made me realize how much I'd been unlearning—how deeply past relationships, especially the one with the narcissist, had shaped my sense of what was safe. It wasn't that men were inherently untrustworthy; it was that I had stopped trusting anyone at all. I had internalized the idea that no one owed me anything, and in turn, I didn't owe anyone either. It was all self-protection—armoring up against vulnerability, calling it independence.

But trust doesn't mean certainty. It doesn't mean blind faith. It means choosing openness, even when the outcome is unknown. It means saying, "This is how I feel," and letting that be enough without demanding promises or guarantees. That night, in the simplicity of that exchange, I realized I was finally learning to trust again. Not just in someone else, but in my own ability to navigate whatever came next.

So, when I set out on my trip, I felt a surprising sense of calm leaving this new relationship behind. Not because I didn't care about him, I did, but because I finally felt grounded enough in myself not to need certainty. There was no pressure to define what we were or make promises we weren't ready for.

Still, as much as I liked him, I'm not blind to the realities of travel. When you're thousands of miles away, in foreign countries, surrounded by fellow wanderers, it's natural for new connections to form. And as someone who's always been a bit of a lover girl at heart, I've learned not to resist these moments. If romance finds me, I welcome it.

There was Frey, the fun Swede who reminded me not to shrink life into routines and permanence. He was the one I mentioned who made the fleeting feel full and that magic exists inside the mundane. And then there was Christian, the wild Australian I met on a party boat in Croatia. I somehow convinced him I was Australian too and spent our entire time together faking an accent. We danced through bars and boat decks like we had been a couple for years.

I let myself enjoy the lightness of those connections. Each one was brief, beautiful, and unforgettable in its own way. But I also surprised myself. I didn't let the romance go further than a few kisses and some late-night conversations under the stars. And for me, that was a big deal. I cared about Joshua. I respected what we were building—even in its early, undefined form—enough to protect it.

One night, tipsy and sun-warmed from dancing, I sent him a message.

"I'm gonna be honest, I could have slept with someone last night. But all I want is you."

His reply came a few moments later.

"Honestly that's hard to believe."

"Yeah, I know…Trust me."

There it was. *Trust.* The word landed with more weight than I expected. He knew my history. Knew that travel romances were kind of…my thing. I had a pattern, and we both knew it.

"Okay…"

"You don't believe me?"

"Trust is something earned, and that can only be proven through time. I'm not saying I doubt you—but essentially, just saying: we'll see."

"Fair enough," I replied. "Well, I'll always tell you the truth. No matter what."

He softened a little.

"You seem honest enough to me. Based on the conversations we've had and your character. You've given me no reason not to trust you."

There was something about him acknowledging my *character*—not just my words, not my behavior in that moment, but the core of who I was—that struck me. It caught me off guard in the best way. I felt this sudden surge of pride. Not for being "good" or "loyal," but being seen, really seen, by someone I was growing close to.

And that's when it hit me: I had never fully trusted my own character until someone else reflected it back to me.

It wasn't that I didn't know who I was. Deep down, I did. But I had been carrying so much doubt, and so many old stories from past relationships that made me question my worth, my loyalty, my capacity to be truly seen.

But his words made something click. The way we perceive ourselves eventually mirrors how others perceive us, too. And in that moment, I realized I was finally secure not just in our relationship, but in myself. That sense of security was being reflected back to me through his trust, his recognition of my character.

And that—*that* was healing.

After I had completed the solo part of my journey, I FaceTimed G from London and told her everything. How proud I felt. How I could feel myself growing in real time, finally healing from all the tangled trauma I had carried into my past relationships. I told her how Joshua's words stirred something I hadn't expected but clearly needed to hear. It shifted something internal—something foundational.

For the first time in a long time, I wasn't chasing trust from someone else to feel secure. I was building it within myself.

And that's what brought me to the most unexpected and oddly comforting realization:

The world doesn't care about you.

And that's... *liberating*.

You, me, everything we do—it will all one day be forgotten. It'll be like we were never here, even though we were. And yeah, that might sound bleak at first. But really, it's kind of the best news ever. It means you're free.

Nobody is watching you as closely as you think they are. Nobody is keeping score. People are far too wrapped up in their own lives, their own insecurities, their own shit, to obsess over yours for long. Most of the things you think people will judge you for? They won't even remember.

And once you realize that something wild happens:

You get your freedom back.

Being okay with the world not caring about you is what allows you to exercise your free will in its purest form. You stop performing. You start choosing. You start creating a life that feels like yours and not one shaped by fear, approval, or imaginary expectations. It's where authenticity begins.

Humans didn't evolve to be the strongest or the fastest or even the smartest species on Earth. We rose to the top because of one remarkable trait: our ability to collaborate. Across millions of years, entire parts of our brain have developed solely for the purpose of navigating relationships, reading social cues, and fitting in. Belonging has always been key to our survival.

This wiring is what makes us so effective at working together toward a shared goal. But it's also what makes us so vulnerable to shame, comparison, and fear. The same instincts that help us build communities also cause us to obsess over our perceived flaws, to replay conversations in our heads, to shrink ourselves to avoid standing out.

And yet—it's a superpower.

When you stop obsessing over how you're being perceived and instead focus on presence and connection, everything changes. People open up. They feel seen. They laugh more. And so do you.

Because when you stop performing and start *being*, people don't just respond, they *relate*. And in that space, trust begins to build. Not from how perfectly you're perceived, but from how truthfully you show up.

One of my best friends, Eric, is the king of free will. Born and raised in Portland, Oregon, to Vietnamese immigrant parents, he grew up surrounded by creativity, culture, and open-mindedness. Portland—at least the version he came of age in—was a place where weirdness was celebrated, where people experimented with identity, where marching to the beat of your own drum wasn't just accepted, it was expected.

So, when Eric chose to spend seven years in the Midwest for college and graduate school, he was met with a very different lifestyle. The Midwest wasn't Portland. It was much more reserved. People didn't push boundaries in the same way. Instead, they respected and upheld them. Tradition and family ran deeper. There was a subtle pressure to fit in, to go with the grain, to avoid standing out too much.

And for Eric—an openly gay man and a person of color—being in that environment added an entirely different layer. It wasn't just about adapting to a different pace of life. It was about navigating spaces where parts of his identity weren't always visible, valued, or even safe. He often told me that people weren't necessarily unkind, they just didn't get it. They didn't know how to hold space for those who lived loudly and outside their narrow frame of reference.

I understood that more than I could put into words. Because I've seen it, too.

There's a particular kind of life that's considered *ideal* in many Midwestern towns—one that follows a reliable script. You get your degree. You find a partner. You settle down. You buy a house. You show up to tailgates and birthday parties and bottomless brunches. You're friendly. And predictable. And polite. You don't make people uncomfortable with your politics, your pain, your past. There's a beauty in that simplicity—comfort, even.

And to be clear, this isn't to shit on the Midwest.

There's nothing wrong with wanting that life. For some people, it's exactly the right fit. It's wholesome and grounding. But for people like Eric and for people like me, it also felt like confinement.

I didn't grow up in the Midwest, but I spent enough time there to know what it feels like to want something more and be met with polite confusion. To feel like ambition, creativity, or intensity makes you a little bit "too much." I remember feeling guilty for wanting more than what was in front of me. For wanting to be somewhere else not because I didn't love the people around me, but because I knew I wasn't the most authentic version of myself.

Eric and I have always bonded over that. Our environments didn't reflect who we were or who we were becoming, and that dissonance was what eventually pushed both of us to make bold moves. For him, it was New York. For me, it was London.

I remember a call from him one day while he was finishing his PA degree in Milwaukee. He was venting about how ready he was to leave. He told me how much he appreciated the Midwest for what it gave him, but how exhausting it had become to constantly feel like he had to dim his light. "I'm just tired of feeling like I have to dress down my personality around people who are just…basic," he said, half-joking.

It hurt to hear that. I could tell he was feeling low, like he wasn't being fully seen, and maybe starting to forget how vibrant he really was.

But later that day, he texted me:

"I had a change in mindset. Why the fuck am I debating staying at home all day, when nothing's happening inside. I put on an outfit that's way too good for Milwaukee because I owed it to myself. Took my ass out, finished my presentation, enjoyed the sun, and ended up at a cannabis bar next to my place."

"I literally love free will."

That's it, right there.

My closest college friends and I have started sending photos in our group chat of us exercising our *free will*. It's our way of celebrating the small, ridiculous, entirely unnecessary choices that make life fun. Someone might send a selfie with a margarita at 2 p.m. on a Tuesday. Another might send a picture from bed at four in the afternoon with the caption, *Haven't moved all day*. Sometimes it's booking a last-minute trip, sometimes it's wearing something outrageous just because, sometimes it's choosing to do absolutely nothing at all.

Free will isn't just about the big, life-changing decisions—moving cities, quitting jobs, or ending relationships. It's in the micro-moments. The tiny, ordinary choices you make when no one's watching and no one's keeping score.

It's in deciding you're going to have a good day before it happens. It's in wearing something that makes you feel good, even if you'll only see strangers. It's in choosing to take yourself somewhere new simply because you want to. It's in honoring your own desires without first asking if they're practical, reasonable, or "deserved."

We tend to think of free will as the freedom to change the course of our lives. And yes, it's that—but it's also the freedom to inhabit your life fully, exactly as it is. It's the ability to say, *This is my one day on Earth, and I'm not going to waste it pretending to be less than I am.*

That's the way Eric lives his life. It's what makes his presence magnetic. He reminded me that the world might not care, but you should. You owe it to yourself to show up not for attention, or applause, but because you can. Because no one else gets to decide how much of you is too much.

And somehow, that looped me right back to Joshua.

It's funny how healing rarely happens in the way you expect. I thought I'd find self-trust in solitude. On a mountain. Or a retreat. Through some dramatic act of independence. But it found me in a text conversation. In a partner's confidence in who I was. In the simplicity of being seen and being trusted for it.

That trust wasn't something I needed from him. It was something I was finally ready to receive because I had started to believe in myself.

I realized I wasn't trying to prove anything more. Not to him, not to anyone. I wasn't living like someone terrified of messing up or being misunderstood. I wasn't negotiating my worth through other people's perceptions.

That's what self-trust looks like. Not perfection. Not control. Just choosing to stay true to yourself, even when the outcome is uncertain. Especially then.

And here's the part that still amazes me: once I stopped anxiously asking: *Can I trust them?* I started confidently asking: *Can I trust me?*

And the answer, finally, was yes.

And the answer for you is *yes,* too.

Yes—you can trust yourself to tell the truth.

Yes—you can trust yourself to walk away when something no longer feels right.

Yes—you can trust yourself to love fully, knowing you'll survive even if it ends.

Yes—you can trust yourself to begin again.

That's freedom. Not living a life free from judgement but living one that's free from the *fear of it.* Not because the world is watching—but because it's not.

And when you really let that truth in, when you stop needing the world to care in order to care for yourself, that's when everything changes.

Because the world doesn't care.

And that's not something to grieve.

It's something to rise into. It means you're in the clear. The pressure is off. It means you get to choose who you want to be— and then be them, unapologetically.

That's liberation.

Chapter 15: No-Wake Zones

Dear Reader,

If you've ever been on a boat, you know how smooth it can feel when you're the one at the helm. From where you sit, it's all control and clarity. The engine hums, the horizon calls, the water parts obediently beneath you. You lean into the speed, its cadence, the freedom. But you don't feel the wake. You don't feel the ripples stretching far beyond you, rocking the anchored boats, unsettling the paddle boarders, spilling someone's coffee on a dock. To you, it's just motion. To everyone else, it's turbulence.

Life often works the same way. We become absorbed in our own forward momentum—our desires, ambitions, moods, or worries—and in that absorption, we forget how easily our actions radiate outward. What feels like a throwaway comment to us may sit with someone for days. A careless decision can leave those tethered to us scrambling to steady themselves. Our inner calm, or our inner chaos, spreads whether we intend it to or not.

The thing about wakes is they don't stop when the boat does. They keep rolling, bouncing off shorelines, colliding with other waves, carrying an impact long after we've forgotten we made it. The same is true of the wake we leave in the lives around us. Sometimes it's subtle—a ripple of kindness, a smile that steadies someone who was sinking. Other times it's sharp and jarring. The kind of wave that knocks the wind out of someone who never saw it coming.

The question is not whether you create a wake. You do. We all do. The real question is whether you're aware of it. Whether you're the kind of captain who speeds through the no-wake zone, insisting the rules don't apply, or the kind who eases off the throttle, mindful of who else shares the water. Because the wake we leave behind us is, in many ways, our truest signature. Not the course we set, not the speed we travel, but the way we ripple into the lives around us.

***

My dad owned a boat up on Lake Granby, Colorado, throughout my high school years. Lake Granby is the third-largest body of water in the state, fed by the cold, clear inflows of the Colorado River. In the summers, our family would pack up and head there on weekends, escaping the heat of the city for the crisp air of the Rockies. Just forty-five minutes from Winter Park, the lake stretched wide and glittering, ringed by pine-covered hills and distant peaks still capped with snow even in July.

Those weekends are some of my fondest memories during my teen years. We'd spend mornings paddle boarding across the still water, afternoons tubing until our arms ached from holding on. And some days, we would simply boat in circles for hours not to get anywhere, but just to be out on the water, tracing the eleven-mile expanse, and watching the sun tilt toward the horizon. There was something timeless about those rides, a movement and stillness that seemed to suspend the ordinary pace of life. It was a kind of family time that only existed out there on the lake, wrapped in the sounds of the motor and the endless shimmer of water.

Weekends in Granby were also some of the happiest I ever saw my dad. An east-coaster at heart, he carried with him a longing for the ocean he had left behind. Being on the water, even a mountain lake nearly 9,000 feet above sea level, seemed to bring him back to himself, and back to the peace of his roots. It gave him not just the calm of the water but also the joy of sharing it with his family.

For him, those weekends became a perfect blend of fatherhood and homecoming. They were a chance to bond with us, but especially with my younger brother, Dominick. Dad and Dom had their own ritual: waking up earlier than the rest of us, slipping quietly out of the condo before dawn, and making their way down to the dock. By the time the sun crested the ridgeline and spilled its first gold across the lake, they would already be out on the water, rods in hand, their boat cutting a line through the morning stillness. For them, those hours of fishing were less about the catch and more about the companionship—the kind of easy silence and shared presence that only fathers and sons know.

Looking back, I can see how profoundly impressionable those years were for our entire family. Granby was a place where we knew who we were together. We were siblings laughing as we took turns tubing, parents watching proudly form the stern, the lake itself holding us in a kind of summer sanctuary. It was family distilled to its simplest and truest form.

But like all seasons, those summers had to end. By the time I was graduating and preparing to head off to college, the boat had to be sold. Dad made the difficult decision to let it go to help cover the costs of my tuition—a sacrifice that I know was hard to make. And as the "boat years" ended, life began to transition. We grew older, our schedules scattered, and the nature of our relationships began to shift.

Our family bond was never static; it has always evolved with us. My relationship with my parents was not the same as Dom's, and neither of ours mirrored that of our other siblings. Each of us carved a different connection with them, as if our family was a web of distinct yet intertwined relationships. We all found new ways of relating to each other, new forms of connection that reflected who we were becoming in those years of transition.

By the time I was packing for college, G and Dom were just entering their high school years. It's only in hindsight that I see how difficult it must have been for them to navigate that season without me. At the time, I was consumed with my own excitement, blinded by the thrill of stepping into independence. For G and Dom, my absence meant facing the turbulence of adolescence with one less anchor at home. They had each other, being only seventeen months apart, which gave them a built-in ally. But Christian and I were gone, and Joey was still too young to connect with them in any meaningful way.

As close as they were, that closeness often got them into trouble. They moved through those years like co-conspirators, bound together in loyalty but also in recklessness. Meanwhile, I was hundreds of miles away, busy partying in dorm rooms, reveling in freedoms I had never known before. My world was expanding outward while theirs was collapsing inward.

And then the phone calls would come. I can still remember the sound of my mom's voice on the other end of the line tight with exhaustion, thick with tears, as she told me G and Dom were out of control. They had started experimenting with substances, getting involved with troubled peers, and treating the adults in their lives with open disrespect. From my dorm room miles away, I felt both distant and entangled, caught between two worlds: the one I was building for myself, and the one I had left behind.

I grew angry with them—so upset that they were causing my parents so much tribulation. Each call from my mom left me frustrated, not only at their behavior but at the ripple effect it had on all of us. And instead of leaning in with compassion or trying to embrace them by listening and seeking to understand, I became resentful. I slipped into the role of the know-it-all big sister, speaking to them less like a sibling and more like a third parent.

It was easier, in some ways, to scold from a distance than it was to sit with their reality. I told myself I was holding them accountable, when in truth, I was guarding myself and shielding against the discomfort of their pain and their struggles. I forgot what it felt like to be sixteen, confused and restless, searching for belonging in all the wrong places. I forgot that what they needed most was not another lecture, but someone willing to sit with them in the mess and to remind them they weren't alone.

But distance can harden empathy. From the outside, it was simpler to see their actions as failures rather than cries for help. And so, I carried resentment instead of grace, authority instead of compassion. In my eyes, they had stopped being my two baby siblings who once followed me everywhere, copying everything I did the way younger siblings do. Somewhere along the way, that stage had ended.

Their lives took on a kind of mythic quality. I would tell my closest friends at college about their latest escapades—the wild parties they threw back home, the strange trap music thumping through their speakers, the antics that seemed larger than life. Their stories became entertainment, something I recounted over late-night Domino's pizza or in crowded dorm rooms.

It was strange. G and Dom's actions were so out of the ordinary that they turned into characters not just in my life, but in my friends' lives too. People who had never met them felt like they knew them, laughed at their stories, shook their heads at their chaos. The two of them became a kind of legend in absentia— colorful, unpredictable, almost fictional. Yet behind those stories were two real teenagers living through choices and consequences that were far more complicated than the anecdotes I used to make my friends laugh.

Thankfully, after many hard lessons learned, both of them began to mature and slowly outgrow the antics that had caused my parents, and all of us, so much stress. G began to turn inward, centering herself in her spirituality. She found grounding in yoga, in meditation, and in the long, sometimes painful work of self-exploration and actualization. Her steadiness grew alongside a confidence that came not from rebellion but from self-knowledge. It marked the start of her journey into the wise woman she continues to evolve into today.

Dom, on the other hand, leaned fully into his entrepreneurial streak, entering what he proudly calls his "businessman era". But watching him, I couldn't help thinking it wasn't an era at all; it was, and always had been, who he really is. He carried that same boldness that once fueled late-night madness and redirected it into ambition, risk-taking, and a desire to prove himself to the world. For him, growing up meant hustling, chasing ideas, and carving out an identity that was uniquely his own.

Kicked out of high school at fourteen, Dom enrolled in an alternative program that let him take college-level courses; by seventeen he had earned an associate's degree in business. While stacking those credits, he co-founded an LLC and attracted investors to launch his "Cgo" project—attachable magnetic phone batteries—and used the profits to help feed more than 3,000 unhoused people around Denver. When a business deal with those same investors soured, he paid them back by throwing parties across the country. It was audacious and a little unbelievable, but it worked, and it said everything about the way he turned setbacks into momentum.

Despite two horrific car accidents just six weeks apart, Dom didn't stop. The crashes left him with chronic back pain and a long trail of lawsuits, doctors' visits, and rehab. But he redirected the same stubborn energy into the auto world—flipping and reselling cars—while enrolling at Creighton University (my alma mater) to pursue a bachelor's in economics.

By the time he was twenty, he was juggling more than many people do in a lifetime. Contracts and titles, classes and exams, margins and mechanics—all of it layered on top of the relentless toll of his health. He cycled through stem cell therapy, discogram procedures, injections, and finally a spinal fusion surgery, yet somehow kept building, learning, and pushing forward.

Today, Dom continues to excel in his business ventures. He bought a dealership and formed an auto LLC in Omaha, Nebraska, while simultaneously setting up three companies in Honduras. From there, he began stitching together dealership networks, rental fleets, and export routes stretching from Florida to Roatán, the island off the coast of Honduras, and onto the mainland. He learned the intricacies of customs the hard way, navigating paperwork, delays, and negotiations across multiple ports. He kept fleets of cars and jet skis running, built out rental operations for the growing tourism sector, and created jobs for dozens of people. What began as hustle slowly transformed into management across systems, networks, and strategy. Dom was no longer just chasing motion; he was directing it.

But if you only follow Dom on social media and aren't one of the people working with him behind the scenes, you'd probably think his life is nothing but leisure. To the outside world, it looks like he's just partying in random cities, spending his summers on an island, boating from cove to cove, and posing with flashy cars.

I always know when Dom is up to something new and outrageous because one of my friends will text our group chat with messages like, *"Bella, where is Dom now?"* Or *"WHAT is Dom doing?"* Or simply, *"Bella—Dom's story."* His feed makes him less like my brother and more like a recurring character in everyone else's lives.

But what those snapshots don't reveal is the constant stress running quietly underneath it all for me and the rest of our family. The not knowing what Dom might be getting into next. The protective instincts that kick in even when we're miles away. It's insane, yes, and in many ways it makes me proud to be his sister. But it's also a lot to carry when people on the outside are constantly asking what the hell he's doing, while most of us on the inside don't even know half the time.

It's also led to a strange sort of tension between all our independent relationships with him. My brother is one of the most sensitive, kind-hearted, and loyal people you will ever meet. He is also one of the most headstrong, stubborn, and tenacious. Those qualities don't cancel each other out. In fact, they exist side by side, creating a push and pull that is often hard to reconcile when you're close to him.

On one hand, his loyalty and tenderness make you feel seen in a way few people can. He will defend you, care for you, and stand by you with unwavering devotion. On the other hand, his determination can harden into a wall, and his refusal to bend can leave you exhausted, feeling like you're fighting a current you can't redirect. That mix between his deep kindness and his relentless drive means he can break your heart and inspire you in the same breath.

When it's a sibling, that tension cuts even sharper. You know the softness at his core, the child you grew up with, and you love him for it. But you also watch as his stubbornness drags him into storms, and you feel powerless to pull him back. Pride and fear live right next to each other, and that paradox is difficult to navigate.

And maybe that's the paradox we all live with when it comes to the people we love most. They are never just one thing; they hold contradictions. The same qualities that make them extraordinary are often the ones that make them difficult. The same fire that gives them strength can also burn those standing closest. Loving someone up close means carrying both truths at once—the admiration and the exhaustion, the pride and the fear, the beauty and the burden.

I see this not just in myself, but in the people who orbit our family, too. One of my best friends, Lexi, has become an honorary member of our family over the last few years. She's been there to celebrate some of our biggest milestones, and she's stood beside us through some of the hardest seasons. Lexi still lives and works in Omaha, which brings us all an immense sense of comfort knowing she has a presence in the same orbit as Dom. We absolutely adore her. She feels less like a friend and more like a sister. So, when she wound up in the hospital with a frightening kidney infection, my first instinct was to send Dom to check on her.

Dom went and spent hours by her side, chatting her ear off and filling the room with stories of his latest adventures. A few days later, when Lexi was home and starting to feel better, I called to check in.

"Yeah, I'm doing much better. It was definitely scary, but it gave me a whole new appreciation for good health. You just never know what can happen to you. We really aren't invincible," she said in her distinct voice, the kind that always makes people stop and listen.

"Good, I'm so glad. I was so scared for you. And I'm glad Dom was able to be there with you," I replied.

"I know, me too. He's so funny. I couldn't tell if it was just the meds, but some of the stories he was telling me—I was like, *what is happening right now?*"

"Hah, yep. Sounds about right." I laughed. "Honestly, he's been driving our family kind of nuts. I don't think he realizes the stress he puts us all under."

"I can totally see that," she said. "Even I was trying to tell him— *look at me right now. You're really only one person, Dom. And one person can only handle so much at once.* I never thought I'd end up in the hospital. I'm young and healthy."

"I know," I sighed. "I don't think he understands that fully. Even with all of his medical stuff, you'd think he'd know how to slow down and appreciate the present moment."

"Yeah, but he kept saying, *I'm not most people. I'm Dom. I'm like a bunch of people all in one.*"

And he has a point. Dom isn't like most people, that's for damn sure, and anyone who knows him knows that too. But what he doesn't seem to understand is that all the energy and momentum it takes to be Dom creates a ripple effect. It doesn't just move him forward; it rocks everyone else who's tethered to his life.

And from Dom's perspective, I know he feels misunderstood— that nobody really "gets him." And maybe we don't. Maybe we can't, not fully. His mind runs faster than most, his tolerance for risk is higher, and his vision stretches further than what the rest of us can always see. To him, our worry probably feels like doubt, our concern like restraint. What we call insane, he might call momentum.

In many ways, Dom's outlook echoes a mindset far bigger than himself. In his 1989 bestseller, *The 7 Habits of Highly Effective People,* Stephen Covey brought into mainstream thought what he called the **have-do-be** mindset. It's the belief that once I *have* the right resources—more money, more time, more connections—then I can *do* what I want, and finally *be* the person I want to become. On the surface, it feels logical and even aspirational. It has since become a common model in business thinking: accumulate capital, build resources, then use them to act in ways that eventually define success. Companies adopt it just as individuals do: "Once we have enough market share, we can do X, and then we'll be Y."

But Covey argues that this order is deeply flawed. It puts fulfillment just out of reach, always contingent on having more first. The result is a cycle of chasing, where the goalpost keeps moving. His alternative was the **be-do-have** paradigm: start with *being*—grounded in values, clarity, and purpose. From that foundation, you naturally *do* the right things, and through those aligned actions, you come to *have* the results that matter most. It shifts success from something outside yourself to something you create from the inside out.

And this isn't just about Dom—it's many of us. In Western culture especially, we are taught to measure our lives by what we can accumulate and achieve. We chase degrees, promotions, salaries, houses, always telling ourselves that once we *have* enough, we'll finally be able to *do* the things we love and *be* the kind of person we want to become. But the danger in that thinking is subtle: it keeps us running, often without noticing the weight it places on us or on the people closest to us.

It's no wonder so many of us are exhausted. We live in a society that glorifies busyness, where packed calendars are worn like badges of honor and rest is often treated as laziness. Success is defined by comparison: how much more we have than the person next to us. The race never ends, because there is always someone richer, smarter, younger, more accomplished. In this way, "have-do-be" isn't just a personal mindset; it's the cultural air we breathe.

Other cultures have taught me how deeply ingrained this is in the West. Traveling abroad, I noticed how different the pace can feel—how presence often matters more than progress, how value is measured in relationships or community rather than productivity. In those moments, I caught glimpses of what it means to begin with *being*. To live fully in the day you're in, not in the imaginary day when you finally "have enough."

But back home, the pressure to achieve is constant. The promise of contentment is always tied to the next ring of the ladder, the next raise, the next accomplishment. It's a culture that doesn't just push us forward but pulls us away from ourselves. And when we're caught in that cycle, it's easy to forget that our striving doesn't happen in isolation. The way we chase, the speed at which we move, always spills over into the lives of others.

That's where the inspiration for this chapter's *Dear Reader* letter first came from. The realization that the momentum we feel inside our own lives is rarely the same as what others experience around us. I had written those words as a reflection, but the wake metaphor itself only came to me recently in a conversation with my parents' best friends, Guy and Renee.

They had come over while my parents were away, stopping by to check on things and savor the end of summer stretched out by our family's pool. The cicadas clicked in the background, and classic rock played just loud enough not to bother the neighbors. As the day settled in, I found myself confiding in them about Dom and the anxieties I carried about never knowing what he might get into next.

Guy sat with his feet dangling in the water, listening quietly, letting me get it all out. Then, after a pause, he leaned back and said, almost casually, "You've gotta think of it like a boat and its wake. The person driving never feels it, but everyone else does."

The simplicity of it hit me like a truth I already knew. Suddenly, I was back at Lake Granby, watching my dad's boat trace circles across the eleven-mile stretch of water. From inside the boat, everything felt smooth, steady. But if you were out on a paddle board, or sitting on the dock, you felt every wave that churned behind it. The driver never notices the wake; only those around them do.

That image stayed with me because it fit Dom so perfectly, especially knowing how much joy he found in those days on the lake with our dad. To him, life feels like forward motion enthralled with momentum and control. To the rest of us, it feels like being rocked by waves we never asked for, scrambling to keep balance while he speeds toward the horizon. And yet, when I think of Lake Granby, I don't only remember the wakes. I also remember the stillness of the glassy mornings when the water mirrored the mountains, when nothing disturbed the surface. That stillness is what I long for sometimes, both in him and in myself: the chance to exist without turbulence, to simply *be*.

Talking with Guy reminded me that wakes are inevitable. None of us move through life without leaving ripples. The question is not whether we create them, but whether we are aware of them. Dom may never feel the waves he sets off, just as the driver of a boat rarely notices the turbulence in their trail. And truthfully, most of us don't either. We race ahead, focused on our own speed, our own direction, assuming the ride is smooth. We end up forgetting that someone else may be out there, clutching for balance in the wake we leave behind.

Our striving, our momentum, even our love, can unsettle those closest to us. And yet, the same energy that disrupts can also inspire. The same force that rocks the water can carry others forward if it's guided with awareness.

I love my brother with as much unconditional love as any sibling should. In many ways, I wish more people could possess the same level of spontaneity and self-determination that Dom does. He reminds us that limits are often illusions, that reinvention is always possible, that becoming is a lifelong process. And yet, it's not just about chasing possibility—it's about grounding yourself in value, in being. Because when you start there, the potential you unlock flows with more intention, and it shines in the most glorious ways.

The real work, then, is not to stop moving, not to abandon ambition, but to learn how to steer with care. To recognize that the way you move through the world will always ripple outward. And to ask yourself, in every season: *Am I leaving behind turbulence? Or am I leaving behind something others can ride?*

Chapter 16: Lovers, Not Fighters

Dear Reader,

There is too much fighting in this world. Too much hate disguised as power, too much anger mistaken for strength. I feel it every time I scroll through the news, every time another headline reminds us of how quickly we turn against one another, how deeply we've normalized conflict as the only way forward.

But here's the painful truth: so often, the battles we fight aren't even ours. The rich and powerful—the top one percent—benefit from a divided world. They pit us against each other to distract us from the systems that keep them on top. They whisper stories of scarcity and competition, convincing us that the enemy is our neighbor, our coworker, the stranger across the border—when the enemy is the illusion that we must fight at all. They profit from our fear, while we spend our lives caught in battles that were never truly ours to begin with.

And yet, even knowing this, it's so easy to get swept into the cycle. To armor up. To match hardness with hardness. To believe the only way forward is through combat. But I don't believe we were made for this constant war. Not with each other, and not with ourselves.

I believe we were made to love. To soften where the world has hardened us. To choose tenderness over control, creation over destruction, connection over division.

I believe we were meant to be lovers, not fighters.

***

My mom took me to my first dance class when I was just two years old. Tiny tights stretched over my legs, pink slippers clinging to my feet, a butterfly clip wobbling in my hair because I barely had enough for a real ponytail. I had been raised on the periphery of the dance floor—watching older girls soar across hardwood in clean lines, their ponytails slicing the air, their faces frozen in practiced smiles I'd eventually learn how to hold. Dance was the language I learned before words ever made sense. My mom lived her life in motion; as a former Rebel Girl and Vegas pool girl turned psychologist and educator, movement was her native tongue. I grew up speaking it too. It taught me early that life wasn't linear but rhythmic and cyclical, a choreography of opposites moving together.

That's probably why my life has always felt like a series of intertwined contrasts. I've danced with grief and danced with love, with solitude and belonging, with heartbreak and renewal. Each phase carried its own cadence. The moments that broke me opened new places for healing. Loneliness made connection feel like grace. Freedom revealed longing; longing revealed home.

The law of polarity says everything exists in pairs—light and shadow, joy and sorrow, beginnings and endings. These opposites don't cancel each other out; they create meaning. They're how we learn how to feel. They're what keep us awake.

I saw this play out one night in Denver, out with old high school friends celebrating my friend Erin's move to Chicago. We hadn't seen each other in years, yet the moment we gathered, time unfolded in on itself. We laughed outside the bar about how much we'd grown since those bright-eyed days, and then stepped back into the pulsing haze of the dance floor. The DJ's bass thumped through our chests, pulling us into a crowd of strangers.

Then chaos erupted. A brunette brushed past a blonde, shoulder to shoulder, and before I could process what had happened, the blonde spun around, livid. Words were exchanged, sharp and heated, and suddenly they were shoving, clawing, both throwing punches and kicks while the brunette's boyfriend tried to hold her back. It was absurd, like a fight scene that didn't belong in the middle of what had been such a joyful night.

When the blonde staggered back near me, I reached for her shoulder, trying to calm her down. "It's not worth it," I told her, leaning in close so she could hear me over the music. "Just let it go. Someone like that isn't worth throwing hands over." She couldn't hear me, or maybe she chose not to. The two carried on until they were eventually removed from the dance floor.

My friend Hannah and I looked at each other and immediately burst into laughter. "WTF was that?" We mouthed at the same time, shaking our heads. The fight had been so ridiculous that all we could do was laugh, shrug it off, and keep dancing.

Five minutes later, in the exact same spot where fists had been flying, a small dance circle formed around a bride and groom celebrating their wedding night. They stepped into the center, glowing and joyful, as the crowd cheered them on. The shift was instantaneous, jarring, beautiful. Aggression was replaced by celebration, anger replaced by love.

Hannah leaned over to me, wide-eyed. "That was so crazy. Two back-to-back moments, complete opposites."

"Right?" I said. "It literally went from fighters to lovers."

She laughed, and we kept dancing with the crowd.

And in that moment, the law of polarity wasn't just a theory, it was pulsing through the bass, unfolding on the dance floor, showing me again that life is always both. But the question is: which energy do we allow to lead us?

Spirituality has always been a part of my life, though its shape has shifted many times. I grew up Catholic—attending Mass on Sundays, receiving my First Communion, and later going to a high school and university where theology was written into the core curriculum. But as the years passed, I found myself questioning the Church as an institution. I struggled with the rigidity of its teachings and the narrow path it prescribed toward the "Divine." There were moments in my life when I felt a presence I might have once called God, but those moments never arrived through doctrine or in homilies. They came in ways the Church didn't seem to always recognize. And so, I began to distance myself—not from God, but from the idea of God I had been given. I believed in a love far greater, more expansive, and more intimate than the one I was taught, and I followed that love inward.

As I traveled and read and questioned, I discovered that nearly every spiritual and philosophical tradition has its own language for the same truth: we are always balancing two energies—masculine and feminine, structure and flow, intellect and intuition. Yet the world I grew up in privileged one half of the equation.

The modern world, in so many ways, is built almost entirely on masculine-coded values: productivity over presence, achievement over embodiment, logic over feeling, certainty over curiosity, domination over connection, speed over introspection. We celebrate hustle and call it virtue; we treat vulnerability as weakness; we reward those who push through rather than those who listen inward. Even the way we measure worth—through output, efficiency, discipline—leans toward a version of power that suppresses anything fluid or uncontained. And in that imbalance, the feminine didn't just disappear—it was dismissed.

Even Mary Kassian, a conservative Catholic whose views differ from mine entirely, speaks to this loss in her own way. In *The Feminist Mistake,* she argues that modern culture didn't just empower women—it restricted the meaning of femininity itself. Kassian warns that feminism has not "promot[ed] a healthy self-identity for women," but has instead created "gender confusion," conflict, and a dismantling of the morality and family structures she believes were God-designed. To her, femininity has become untethered from tradition, stretched too far, and unmoored from the boundaries that once defined it.

I don't share her conclusions. I don't believe femininity is fragile, nor do I believe it collapses under the weight of modernity. It expands. It evolves. It breathes. It is not a power meant to be confined or protected behind walls.

But I do believe Kassian touches on something real. When she speaks of a culture that has "lost the feminine," I agree—just not in the way she means it. The feminine wasn't lost because women changed; it was lost because we shrank it. Because we treated the feminine as something that belonged only to women, rather than recognizing it as an energy that exists within all of us. Where Kassian sees the unraveling of tradition, I see the unraveling of something deeper: a spiritual imbalance that predates politics entirely.

For generations, femininity has been silenced in all of us, regardless of gender. And yet, despite our differing beliefs, Kassian and I meet in a shared ache: a recognition that something essential has gone missing. Not the social roles of the past, but the spiritual energy beneath them. The tension around the feminine isn't just cultural—it's spiritual. It lives in our bodies, our relationships, our choices, the ways entire civilizations rise or fall depending on which energies they honor or suppress. Every tradition I've studied—religious, philosophical, mystical—seems to whisper the same truth: when we lose touch with the feminine, we lose touch with ourselves.

I didn't know it then, but the clearest example of that erasure— the most literal, devastating, irrefutable one—was waiting for me in a story that had been buried for centuries.

One afternoon, while working in a coffee shop with my friend Clancy, I told her I was trying to write about spirituality and the role of the feminine in my life. She perked up from her computer, nodded, and said, "Oh my gosh you have to listen to this podcast with Meggan Watterson and Glennon Doyle. It talks about the Divine Feminine through the story of Mary Magdalene." And that was how I encountered theologian Meggan Watterson and her research on the Gospel of Mary Magdalene.

When I first heard Watterson describe Mary's gospel—its burial, its suppression, its dangerous beauty—I felt something inside me tighten, then expand. Mary's gospel wasn't excluded accidentally. It wasn't overlooked or forgotten. It was intentionally erased. In the first few centuries after Jesus's death, Christianity wasn't one unified religion. It was a collection of diverse communities, each with different understandings of who Jesus was and what his teachings meant. Some groups emphasized inner knowing; others emphasized hierarchy. Some believed salvation came through awakening; others believed it came through obedience. The early Jesus movement was fluid, decentralized, and radically diverse.

But by the fourth century, the Roman Empire, which had once persecuted Christians, now sought to use Christianity as a tool of political unity. Emperor Constantine and later bishops wanted one narrative, one doctrine, one hierarchy. Unity, to them, meant control. And control required deciding which texts were acceptable and which were too destabilizing.

Gospels like Thomas, Philip, and Mary were deemed dangerous because they taught that the divine was found within, not through an institution. They suggested that no priest, no empire, no hierarchy could gatekeep God. They emphasized awakening in this life, not suffering for a reward in the next. They elevated inner authority over external rule. And Mary Magdalene's gospel, in particular, uplifted a woman as the one with spiritual clarity, the one Jesus trusted with teachings the male disciples couldn't understand. And to an empire consolidating power, this was intolerable.

So, her gospel was buried—literally. Some monks, ordered to destroy it, refused. Instead, they hid it in the sands of Egypt, where it remained for nearly 1,500 years, waiting for a world that might finally understand it.

When Christ appears to Mary in a vision in her gospel, she asks him, "How is it that I am able to see you? Is it with the soul or with the Spirit?" And Christ answers, "Blessed are you for not wavering at seeing me. For where the mind is, there is the treasure." But "mind" in Greek is *nous*—the spiritual eye of the heart. The inner vision. The clarity that comes when we peel back the ego's layers of fear, shame, and confusion. Mary trusted her inner vision. Christ affirmed it. And that alone would have been enough to terrify any structure built on external authority.

The message emphasized in these suppressed gospels is simple, radical, and threatening: there is no hierarchy to God. No gender closer to the divine. No institution that owns the sacred. The kingdom is within. Salvation means to become alive *now*. Not to spend your life suffering in hopes of a future award. Love is the closest thing to power the human heart will ever know, and power that comes from within is impossible for empires to control.

Hearing this felt like a confirmation of everything I had always sensed but never had language for. Love isn't soft; it's subversive. Love isn't weak; it's ungovernable. Love decentralizes power. And love, as Mary Magdalene knew, is the inner authority we've been trained to mistrust.

As I learned more, I began to see that Mary wasn't alone in this message. Across cultures, mythologies, and religious traditions, the feminine archetype—the intuitive, compassionate, receptive force—has often been diminished, but has always represented the path inward. Tara in Buddhism. Shakti in Hindu philosophy. Sophia in Gnostic cosmology. Yin in Taoism. None of these figures overpower the masculine; they complete it. They restore balance where dominance has taken over. They remind us that wholeness is the goal, not hierarchy.

I felt this truth one morning in Da Lat, Vietnam. Christian, Meo Meo, G and I had escaped there for a weekend—a small retreat from the restlessness of Ho Chi Minh City and into the cool breath of a mountain town. Da Lat felt like an exhale. Mist clung to the pine-covered hills as we wound our way toward the Trúc Lâm Monastery. The air carried the scent of wet earth and incense drifted from shrines hidden between the trees. Perched above a shimmering lake, the monastery appeared almost suspended between water and sky. Monks in saffron robes moved along the stone paths with a stillness that felt like prayer.

Inside the temple, G settled into meditation. A monk noticed her and approached with a soft smile, asking if she practiced. When she nodded, he recognized something in her, and invited her into

225

the inner sanctum, a space ordinarily reserved for monks and nuns. Honored, she asked if we could join. The monk agreed.

We passed through a large gate onto the nuns' side of the monastery, where the air felt denser with intention. A nun greeted us and led us through the dining hall, offering a gentle introduction to Zen Buddhist teaching before guiding us deeper into the sanctum: meditation halls, living quarters, hidden gardens where koi ponds glimmered beneath the trees.

And there stood Green Tara, compassion embodied. One foot extended toward the world, lotus in hand, gaze steady and knowing. In reading Mary's gospel, I was reminded of the presence I felt while staring at Tara. It was the same truth that the divine is not far away. It is here. It is intimate. It is inner. And it has always been feminine as much as masculine.

Tara, considered the Mother of all Buddhas, is the living embodiment of the Divine Feminine: wisdom, compassion, and the boundless potentiality that holds both stillness and creation. Her name comes from the Sanskrit root *tr*, meaning "to cross," because she guides beings across the ocean of suffering toward awakening. In her green form, her right hand offers open-hearted generosity; her left holds a blooming lotus—the symbol of emergence, purity, and inner unfolding.

Standing before her, wrapped in incense and mountain air, I saw that Tara was not separate from us; she was a reminder. A mirror. A symbol of the balance we are meant to carry. Buddhism teaches that any being born from a womb contains both masculine and feminine qualities. Tara simply shows us what harmony looks like when we stop resisting our nature.

Her origin story deepens this truth. As a young princess named Yeshe Dawa, monks urged her to pray for rebirth as a man so she could progress further on the spiritual path. She refused. Only those "weak in mind," she said, believed enlightenment depended on gender. She vowed to take female form until all suffering ended—and attained full enlightenment in that very body.

Both Mary Magdalene and Tara were separated by entire civilizations, yet somehow carried the same defiant truth. Mary's gospel was buried because her authority rose from within, because she didn't need a hierarchy or a man's validation to be close to the divine. Tara's enlightenment was questioned because it blossomed in a woman's body; because she refused to conform to the idea that holiness required masculinity. Both women threatened the structures around them simply by claiming what had always been true—that the divine is not gendered, that spiritual authority is not assigned, and that enlightenment is awakened from within, not granted from above. Across continents and centuries, they echoed the same rebellion: the feminine has never needed permission to be sacred.

The more I let these stories, symbols, and histories move through me, the more I realized that spirituality has never been about rising above the world. It has always been about moving into it with an awakened heart. About letting opposites coexist. About loving in a world that teaches fear. About balancing our inner forces so that we don't get swallowed by either extreme. About choosing connection where conflict would be easier. About remembering that the most powerful force we will ever experience is the love we carry inside ourselves.

The world will always offer us reasons to fight—externally or internally. Fear will aways try to masquerade as safety. Power will always try to disguise itself as truth. Oppressive systems will always attempt to control access to the divine. But the divine has never belonged to systems. It has always belonged to us.

When I step back and look at my life—from childhood dance floors to nights out in Denver to mountain sanctums—I see that spirituality has never been something external for me. It's always been a feeling in my body. In contrasts, and in rhythm. In the moments where opposites meet and don't destroy each other but make each other whole.

And if there's anything this chapter, and this book, is meant to offer, it's this: we were meant to be lovers, not fighters. Not because love is simple, but because love is sovereign. Not because love avoids conflict, but because love transforms it. Not because love is passive, but because love is the only power that doesn't require someone else's diminishment to exist.

Mary Magdalene's gospel taught me that love is the most radical, decentralized force on earth. That divine truth lives within each of us. That balance is our birthright. That wholeness is our nature. And that the kingdom we've been taught to look for in the sky has always been beating in our chest.

Because in the end, it doesn't matter what name we call when we reach for the sacred. It doesn't matter if we kneel in a pew, sit in meditation, light incense, or walk barefoot through a field. The Divine has never cared about the form—only the truth. And the truth is always love. The truth is always balance. Every tradition, every scripture, every myth, every mystic has been trying to say the same thing: that the sacred lives in the place where love steadies us, and balance brings us back to ourselves.

Everything else is choreography.

Chapter 17: One Last Love Letter

Dear Reader,

As I sit down to write this final letter, I can't help but think about everything we've walked through together in these pages—grief and heartbreak, friendship and romance, moments of stillness and wild nights that stitched themselves into memory. Each story, each lesson, has been a piece of the puzzle that makes up my twenties so far. And if there's one thing I've learned in all of it, it's this: our world needs more love.

Not just the big, epic kind of love we see in movies, but the compassionate love of showing up for a friend, the brave love of forgiving ourselves, the everyday love of choosing presence over distraction. The kind of love that begins with us and, when tended to, spills outward into the people and places around us.

In these years of stumbling and searching, I've discovered that love is what makes the losses bearable and the joys unforgettable. Love is what gives meaning to our goodbyes, what soothes our grief into gratitude, what turns strangers into family and fleeting encounters into stories we carry for a lifetime.

I don't pretend to have all the answers, and I know I'll spend many more years learning and unlearning what it means to love well. But if there's one truth I'm certain of, it's that love—for ourselves, for each other, for this fragile, crazy world—is the thing that matters most.

So let this final chapter be a reminder: that we are worthy of our own gentleness, that connection is never wasted, and that even in the hardest moments, we can choose to meet life with open hands and open hearts.

With love,

Bella

✳✳✳

I made one of the first major life decisions of my twenties when I chose to take a year off after college instead of going straight into law school, the way I had always intended. Only a week or so had passed since MK's death, and the grief had settled into me in ways that felt both raw and unfamiliar. My friends and I had mourned her passing and celebrated her life in the most beautiful ways we knew how, but as time carried on, life began pressing forward with its relentless questions: *What's next? Where do we go from here?*

It was during a Zoom meeting with an advisor from Denver University's School of Law that the weight of it all came to a head. We were discussing next steps, mapping out my path toward law school, when she stopped mid-sentence. She must have noticed my swollen, tired eyes, the kind that come from days of crying and nights of restless sleep. I didn't know this woman, yet for some reason, I felt inclined to tell her everything—that my older brother had been in a coma for six weeks earlier my senior year, that one of my closest friends had just died, that this had been one of the hardest years of my life.

She was quiet for a long moment, clearly shaken. Then, with sincerity in her voice, she asked gently, "Bella, have you ever thought that maybe you should just take some time off?"

The question startled me. No, I hadn't thought of that. Law school had been the plan, the only plan, the one constant I thought I could cling to. "No, not really," I admitted. "I'm worried if I take a break, I'll never want to go back."

"I understand, sweetie," she said softly. "But law school will always be here. Right now, you need to prioritize yourself. You need to take care of you before anything else."

Her words lifted the heaviest weight off my shoulders. Tears streamed down my face, unrestrained this time, because for the first time since MK's death, I felt permission to stop running forward. It had never occurred to me that stepping back could be an option or that it could even be the right thing to do. That conversation changed the course of my life. It gave me the greatest relief: the realization that I didn't have to have it all figured out, and that it was okay to pause, to breathe, to grieve.

So, I did. I moved back in with my family, picked up shifts bartending at our local country club, and began saving money while sketching out plans to see more of the world. For the first time in years, I allowed myself to live without a rigid timeline, to move at my own pace.

And when I finally set out, the world unfolded before me in ways I couldn't have imagined. From walking the streets of London, to tracing ancient history in Athens, to laughing alongside four Aussie boys in Rome, I began to see that the world I thought I knew was much larger, richer, and more surprising than I had ever believed. Every city and every encounter chipped away at the fear that had once held me back, revealing a version of myself that was braver, freer, and more open to love than I had ever allowed.

Slowly I began to heal old wounds left behind by past relationships, learning to love myself with more grace and patience than I had ever known. For the first time, I stopped treating self-love as an afterthought and started seeing it as the foundation. It wasn't about grand gestures or sudden transformations—it was in the small, daily choices: forgiving myself when I fell short, speaking to myself with kindness instead of criticism, and allowing space for my own becoming.

Gratitude became my anchor. It steadied me when the waves of grief returned and grounded me in the simplest of moments. A sunrise over a city I'd never seen before. A meal shared with strangers in a hostel who felt like family. The sounds of music spilling out from a bar into the streets. Gratitude reminded me to stay awake to the beauty around me, to be present, and to recognize the privilege of getting to live this life.

My most recent solo adventure took me through the cities of Vienna, Prague, Budapest, and Split. It was the first trip I had ever planned with the sole intention of going alone not because I had to, but because I wanted to. There was something freeing about booking the trains, choosing the hostels, and curating the days entirely for myself.

I had traveled solo once before, a year earlier, but under very different circumstances. Then, I was alone because I had to be. I had parted ways with Olly and was left to navigate the unfamiliar by myself. This time was different. This time, solitude wasn't an accident or a consequence; it was a choice. A choice to give myself the space to listen inward, to move at my own pace, and to prove to myself that being alone could feel like abundance rather than loss.

The journey was wonderful in more ways than one. I was finally checking off cities that had long lived at the top of my bucket list. They were places fellow travelers I'd met over the years had raved about, planting seeds of curiosity in me with their stories. Now, I was there, relishing every minute as I wandered through each one.

In Vienna, I immersed myself in the grandeur of the old Habsburg Empire, walking through palaces that had been transformed into museums, their gilded halls echoing with centuries of history. In Prague, I traced cobblestone streets that felt like stepping into a storybook, each square unfolding with its own rhythm of music, art, and memory. In Budapest, I soaked in thermal baths, watching steam rise against the night sky as the Danube glimmered nearby. And in Split, I sat by the sea, tasting foods passed down across generations, feeling the joys of life in a place where history and modernity meet in balance.

And as I wandered through each city, I found myself quietly waiting for a sign—for the next mark I wanted inked onto my skin. I call my right arm my *passport arm*. It's a collection of patchwork memories, each one drawn by an artist from a different corner of the world. From London to Dublin, Sydney to Madrid, each tattoo is more than just ink. It's a reminder. A story.

A way of bearing the places I've been and the people I've met with me, long after the moment has passed.

Every piece is both personal and shared—something I can point to when telling a story, an invitation for others to ask, *What's that one mean? Where did you get it?* It's my map, etched not in paper but in skin, a living record of the ways the world has shaped me.

By the time I reached Budapest, I felt ready for whatever my next "sign" would be. And then, in the middle of an ordinary afternoon, it appeared. A tiny weight brushed against my leg, and I glanced down at my white linen pants to see something small and dark crawling across the fabric. I startled at first—unsure of what had just landed on me—but when I realized it was a ladybug, I couldn't help but smile.

I lowered my left pointer finger to my thigh, letting her crawl gently onto my hand. She was so delicate, her entire body not even the size of my fingernail, yet vibrant and full of life. With my other hand, I pulled out my phone and snapped a picture: her tiny red form in crisp focus, the Budapest Ferris wheel blurred in the background, a symbol of joy and motion behind her stillness. After a moment, I carried her over to a nearby tree and watched as she crawled onto its bark, disappearing back into the world.

The ladybug was more than just a coincidence. In so many cultures, she's a symbol of luck, of love, of protection, of new beginnings. The symbolism these spotted creatures carry date back centuries, with the gist of belief that if a ladybug lands on you, you'll have as many years of good luck as the bug does spots.

The name "ladybug" itself comes from "Beetle of Our Lady," a nod to the Virgin Mary, who, according to legend, answered the prayers of European farmers whose crops were being destroyed. Ladybugs swooped in, devoured the pests, and saved the harvest. Ever since, they've been seen as protectors and bringers of good fortune. To spot one is to be reminded that things are aligning for you in ways you might not yet see—that abundance is close, and that you are supported, even in silence.

That meaning wasn't lost on me in Budapest. I had been waiting for a sign, and here she was tiny, unassuming, yet powerful in what she represented. In her spotted wings I saw a message meant for me that it was safe to trust the process, to stop forcing answers, and to believe that good things were already in motion. What looked like an ordinary moment became extraordinary, not because of the insect itself, but because of the reminder she carried: that love, luck, and protection are always closer than we think.

And those three things—love, luck, and protection—are things that I believe are often lost when we start to feel disconnected from ourselves and from others. When we forget to nurture our own hearts, or when we drift away from community, it becomes harder to recognize that these forces are still there, still waiting to ground us.

So much of what we crave in our twenties, and really in life, comes back to belonging. It's no wonder that the American university experience is often described as the "best four years of your life." It's not because of the classes or even the freedom. It's because, for a brief moment, we are part of something bigger than ourselves. There's a built-in community: roommates who become family, friends who show up unannounced, a web of connection that holds us together without us even realizing it.

But as we grow older, that structure often fades. The built-in rituals of gathering disappear. Life scatters us across cities, jobs, and timelines that rarely align. And with that scattering, we can start to feel isolated—like love, luck, and protection are slipping away. What we forget is that these things don't vanish with age; they simply require more intention. They ask us to cultivate them in our relationships and our environments, to create community where it doesn't already exist, and to offer others the same safety and belonging we're searching for ourselves. Because so much of who we are—our resilience, our joy, our ability to heal—stems from the relationships we build to ourselves, to others, and to the world around us.

I was visiting my friend Nick in New York when we went to see his office at the One World Trade Center. As soon as we stepped onto the grounds, a surreal energy swept over me. I was too young to remember 9/11 as it unfolded, but I have always understood that it marked a before and after. There was a line in history that forever changed the way we see the world. Standing seventy floors up, looking down at the memorial pools where the Twin Towers once stood, I realized there are some experiences that simply defy words.

What struck me most wasn't just the scale of the building, or the skyline stretched out around us, but the stillness of the memorial below. Even in one of the busiest cities in the world, people gathered in silence, tracing their fingers along the names etched in stone. Strangers moved peacefully around each other, bound not by familiarity but by remembrance. You could feel the weight of loss in the air, yes, but you could also feel the weight of love. It was the kind that brought a broken city, and a shaken world, back together.

That sense of community, of shared grief and shared humanity, hasn't disappeared in the more than twenty years since. It lives in the energy of the space itself. It reminded me that even when tragedy scatters us, there is a way we come back. Love and protection don't evaporate; they remain in memory, in ritual, in the ways we continue to show up for one another long after the immediate crisis has passed.

And it made me think: if such resilience can be built in the wake of something so devastating, then surely, we can find ways to keep building it in our everyday lives. Because like all creatures, humans are creatures of habit. We don't just form routines around brushing our teeth or brewing our coffee. No; we also form habits in how we connect, how we grieve, how we gather, how we love. After 9/11, the habit of showing up through lighting candles, donating blood, and cooking meals became second nature for millions of people. It was instinctual, a rhythm of community.

But with time, and without intention, those rhythms can fade. We fall back into the busyness of life, into the self-contained cycles of work and routine. We have habitual ways of speaking, of listening (or not listening), of reaching out (or withdrawing). And if we're not careful, those defaults become the norm. We stop initiating, stop checking in, stop showing up. And when that happens, even the strongest connections begin to fray.

Psychologist Ian Newby-Clark argues that habits free up mental energy, letting us move through much of our day without having to overthink each action. He uses the examples of "grabbing the milk," "walking the same route," or "sitting at the table and eating toast without noticing." It's efficient, but it also means our social habits—our patterns of communication and intimacy—can slip onto autopilot. And if we don't nurture them, relationships become like gardens left untended: wild, overgrown, distant.

Looking back, I realize this was the undercurrent of so many moments I've written about in this book. Grief taught me that love doesn't end, but carrying it forward requires intention—making a habit of remembering, of celebrating, of saying "I love you" while we can.

Heartbreak showed me how easily toxic patterns become habits too, and how hard, but necessary, it is to rewire them into something healthier.

Travel reminded me that openness itself can be a habit: walking through foreign cities, striking up conversations with strangers, choosing connection even when it's uncomfortable.

Gratitude becomes a habit of presence—a daily practice of pausing long enough to notice beauty in the ordinary, to be awed by what *is* instead of always reaching for what's *next*.

And maybe that's the heart of it: the most important habits are the ones that keep us connected to love, luck, and protection. Not in the abstract, but in the everyday.

Love as a habit of choosing kindness toward ourselves when we falter, and toward others when it's easier to turn away.

Luck as a habit of openness of saying yes, of stepping into the unknown, of trusting that even the smallest encounters can shift our lives.

Protection as a habit of community of showing up, of building the kind of bonds that hold us steady when everything else feels uncertain.

That's what the ladybug reminded me of in Budapest. She wasn't just a sign of luck or protection in some distant, mythical sense. She was a call to practice. To remember that these things don't arrive by chance alone; they grow when we cultivate them. When we make love a habit. When we practice gratitude as presence. When we choose to keep showing up for ourselves and for each other, even in the smallest ways.

And if there's anything I want to leave with you, it's that. Love, luck, and protection aren't fading gifts that come and go with circumstance. They are habits we can live into every single day. Where community isn't lost but rebuilt. Where healing happens not just in moments of tragedy or travel or turning points, but in the ordinary patterns of our lives.

Because in the end, that's what matters most. It's not about how quickly we figure it out or how perfectly we map our futures, but how deeply we love. How much we stay open to grace. How faithfully we show up for each other.

And I can't close without giving thanks to the people who taught me this—to my friends, my family, my community. To the ones who grieved with me, who traveled beside me, who reminded me to laugh when I forgot how. To those who gave me their love in moments when I didn't yet know how to love myself. Your presence has been the greatest proof that love, luck, and protection are not abstract ideas, but living, breathing gifts we give and receive together.

And maybe, if we can remember that, then even the smallest signs—a conversation, a sunrise, a ladybug landing softly on your pants—can remind us of the truth we need most: that love is here, always, and it's ours to give back to the world.

Epilogue

This book began as an attempt to write a love letter to life—to the mess, to the beauty, and everything in between. But no love letter is complete if it only comes from one voice. So, I turned to my family, whose stories are woven into mine, and asked them to join me in this final chapter. I asked them to write me their own love letters to life, and to tell me what they've learned, what they hold close, what keeps them going. These are their answers. Fragments of love, hope, and memory. These are the heartbeat of what carries this story to its end.

Still Becoming by Gianna Scipione

Dear Reader,

Do you know who you are? Do you know where you are? Do you know how you got here? These are questions I stole from the most recent episode of Grey's Anatomy. Cheesy, I know—but hear me out. When my sister asked me to write a letter for her book, I can't lie, I felt panicked. Don't get me wrong—I also felt honored, but mostly panicked. I moved into my own apartment in May. I've been living on my own for five months now, and when people ask me how it's been, I tell them, "It's great! I really love it. It's so nice living on my own. I can wake up in the morning and walk around naked. I can cook breakfast wearing only my socks, and there's nobody around."

There's nobody around.

My sister's book is written on truth—about bravery, courage, and love. It recognizes that our lives are built on connection. So, I'll tell you the real reason why I panicked: because I know myself at my best, and that's when I'm writing. But I haven't written something like this in probably six or seven months—not until I got that text from my sister.

Sure, I get to wake up alone, the sunlight pouring through my floor-to-ceiling windows, vast rays of gold warming the floor of my apartment. But what I don't talk about is that I don't wake up in the morning—I wake up at noon. I don't cook breakfast naked. I wake up, stare at the ceiling for thirty minutes, then scroll through Facebook Reels for another thirty, until that little voice in my head reminds me that I should probably do something considered self-care, so I don't go to work in a bad mood.

I'm 21. I've had a year—almost two—of being in my twenties, and I'm here to share a few things I've learned and reflected on.

Some things I hate about this chapter of life, and others that fill me with a quiet joy at the end of this whirlwind tunnel.

There's something really special about that Grey's Anatomy quote—it feels like the premise of becoming an adult, or rather, a young adult. From what I've experienced so far, I have to be honest: I don't know who I am, or who I'm becoming. I have an idea of the person I want to become, but the path feels daunting.

I'm learning that I want to be a good human—even on the days when I don't feel like being one. That I can't project all of my emotional turmoil onto others just because I'm having a rough month—or a rough five months. That pain is mine to hold, examine, and understand before I can move forward.

It's nobody else's fault but my own that I stay up until 2 a.m. watching Grey's Anatomy because I'm avoiding looking around and seeing all that I've built for myself. I pay for my own apartment. I own my car (thank you, settlement money—and, strangely enough, thank you, car accident). I have friends at work. I have a family that loves me and nurtures our bond. I have a boyfriend I adore and would do anything for.

And yet—some mornings I wake up, look around, and feel so utterly confused about how I got here. I think about my past, about the people I used to surround myself with, and I feel guilt for that sixteen-year-old girl who still lives in me, the one I thought so little of. Now I'm here, and most days, I struggle to face the truth: that everything I have, I am worthy of.

In my twenties, I'm learning to see my worth, to embrace it, and to nurture it. And the simplest truth that keeps me grounded every single day is this: my existence, my being here, on this beautiful planet we all call home, is enough.

Some days, when I can't get out of bed or off the couch, I remind myself that I live in a building surrounded by other buildings full of people just like me. People with partners, people with kids, people who are simply trying. I walk over to my sliding glass door, step out onto the patio, and let the sounds of laughter, cars, and footsteps drift through my apartment. It reminds me I'm not alone—that the only reason I feel alone is because I convince myself that I am.

The joy of being in my twenties is knowing that I will never be this young, this healthy, or this capable again. Every day, we grow older—and while that truth sometimes makes me cry, on the days it doesn't, gratitude rushes through me so strongly it almost hurts.

On those days, I feel the ecstasy of my youth—the wild gift of being human, of watching others live their own lives beside mine. My favorite thing about being twenty-one, about being a soul in this body, is when I realize that I have the superpower to stop time for just a moment—to feel the steadiness of the earth, to witness life and death coexisting, to see it all harmonize into something whole.

It's in those moments that I understand the beauty of the question: Do you know who you are? Do you know where you are? Do you know how you got here?

Because maybe the answer isn't supposed to be clear yet. Maybe the beauty of being in your twenties—of being alive—isn't in knowing the answers, but in learning to ask the questions with wonder instead of fear.

Still Becoming,

G

Forever Your Brother by Christian Scipione

Dear Reader,

I could attempt to wax poetically about the trials and tribulations of navigating one's twenties, but my experience was far from whimsical. The stark reality is that your twenties represent a peculiar juxtaposition of desperately clinging to the vestiges of youth while gradually inching toward what society deems "adulthood." For some, this transition may seem like a seamless journey from university life to graduation, finding a dream partner, and landing a stable job. Regrettably, the contemporary world has rendered that pathway an elusive fantasy, rife with crippling financial burdens, existential crises that strike at 1pm while commuting to work, or at 3am during relentless doom-scrolling.

In today's landscape, we are constantly faced with the dilemma of chasing what we think we should do versus what we genuinely want. It's a messy, confusing time when the lines blur between responsibility and freedom.

I encountered a myriad of challenges from ages 20 to 29. My journey included everything from experiencing homelessness to living in a foreign country, and then finding my way back to the United States, bouncing around rural Indiana, Texas, and the bustling cities of Chicago and Denver. All of this was part of my quest to uncover my identity or perhaps to fill a void I thought was glaring in my existence. Along the way, I met people who mirrored my own struggles—lost but not without purpose, rebellious yet not driven by mere contrarianism. These were individuals who, like me, yearned to understand what all of this truly means.

I spent countless long nights pondering, conversing, and desperately searching for reasons to believe that any of this holds value, grappling with the struggle to find motivation to continue. It often felt easier to say, "none of this matters, so what's the point of even trying?" Yet, it's worth recognizing that many of us find ourselves grappling with a quarter-life crisis more intensely than ever in our twenties, and it's all too easy to feel overwhelmed by a sense of helplessness amidst the chaos. Ultimately, this experience is universal and relatable, reminding us that we are not alone in this wild ride called adulthood.

Americans are often accused of using the word love flippantly. In a way, they may be right. We often go to hyperbolic extremes when describing our hobbies, likes, dislikes and endeavors. However, the ancient Greeks rationalized this concept by adding the suffix "-phile" to the ending of words. Bibliophile—a person who loves books. An Ailurophile—a person who loves cats. And Xenophile—someone who loves foreign customs, traditions or cultures.

We shouldn't be wary of this word or the different connotations it may carry. Love letters don't always need to be romantic in nature. Nowadays far too few people (including myself) take the time to extol about the things they are passionate about. Hell, nowadays passions come and go as quickly as a new Tik-Tok trend or viral meme.

That's why I'm so incredibly proud of my baby sister for taking the long, arduous and painstaking process of writing a book. This is my love letter to her. I hope she knows how much I admire and look up to her as a well-rounded human being at this quarter point of her life. There's no limit to the things she will be able to do, and the people she will inspire along the way. I love you, Tinky.

Forever your Brother,

Christian

Letter to My Younger Self by Dr. Kimberly J. Scipione

Dear Younger Me,

Time is probably the greatest resource we overlook and underappreciate. When you're young, it drags on endlessly—days feel long, and years feel infinite. But as you grow older, you'll realize how quickly it slips away. Appreciate the time you have, because once it's gone, you can never get it back.

I wish you'd spent more time playing with your sister on the farm—laughing, sharing secrets, and being best friends instead of rivals. One day you'll understand how rare and sacred that bond is, and how much joy there is in simply being together.

I wish you'd slowed down in high school and enjoyed learning for the sake of curiosity rather than rushing to work and earn money. There's a lifetime for responsibility, but youth offers only a short season for discovery.

I wish you'd embraced the full college experience—the friendships, the challenges, the freedom to explore. Working hard was noble, but rushing through meant missing moments that could have shaped you in softer, more joyful ways.

I wish you'd played with your children more when they were little—really played, without glancing at the clock or worrying about the laundry, lunches, or spotless rooms. You'll come to realize that those messy, beautiful moments were the ones that mattered most.

I wish you'd traveled more to visit your children in college, to see their lives unfold, to share in their adventures. The work and the career you built will always be there—but their stories, their laughter, and those fleeting chapters will not.

And maybe, I wish you'd saved a little more—gone without the new car or trendy outfit. Not because things matter, but because time does. Saving a little then might have given you more freedom now to savor it.

Time is precious, and only with age will you fully understand that truth. So slow down. Breathe deeply. Look around and really see the people and moments that make your life meaningful. You don't get time back—but you can make the most of the time you have left.

With love and understanding,

Your Older Self

With Warmth & Wisdom by John Scipione

Dear Reader,

As I reflect on my life and the lessons learned over the years, I feel compelled to share not just what I have learned, but also what I wish I had understood when I was in my twenties. These insights might help you navigate the beautiful, messy journey ahead. As a husband of 26 years, father of five, and grandfather to one, I've lived and seen some things.

First, let's talk about what seems important now that won't matter later. In your twenties, you may feel immense pressure to fit in, achieve certain milestones, or appear a certain way. Remember, the opinions of others may weigh heavily on you, but in the grand scheme of life, many of those judgments will fade. The true measure of your life will be the relationships you build and the experiences you savor, not the likes on your social media posts or the designer labels you wear.

And while we're at it, let's not forget that you can't buy more time. The moments you have now are precious; don't take them for granted. Tomorrow isn't guaranteed, and every day is a gift. Be present. Dive into conversations, laugh freely, and don't be afraid to express your feelings. Life is fleeting, and the time spent with loved ones is irreplaceable. When your time on this spinning rock is up, your last words won't be, I wish I had worked more.

You will also discover that there are no entitlements in life, not even your next breath. Each day is a new opportunity, but it can also be a reminder of life's fragility. Approach each moment with gratitude and awareness; it will serve you well.

Seek out conversations with those who have walked the path before you, mentors, family members, or even friends with life experience. Their stories can offer invaluable insights and inspire you to navigate your own journey with wisdom. You might be surprised at how much you can learn from their triumphs and mistakes.

Don't be afraid to fail or feel discouraged by a no. Rejection is part of life, and every setback can teach you resilience. Embrace these challenges; they often lead to growth and new opportunities. Remember, humility is key. You are unique, but you are not so special that you are exempt from the trials of life. Allow yourself to be authentic, and don't shy away from the road less traveled. That path may lead you to the most fulfilling experiences.

In your interactions with others, strive to do no harm. Be kind. Don't spend so much energy and time hating what's different or those not like you. Instead, be a good human. Do something nice for someone just because, even if it's a stranger. Pay it forward without looking for recognition or a pat on the back. Just do the right thing for the sake of it. Be appreciative and respectful to those who wait on and serve you. They are not beneath you regardless of who you think you are. These small acts of kindness can create ripples of positivity that extend far beyond your immediate circle. Have good manners. Please and Thank You, often taken for granted, go a long way.

And most importantly, don't take yourself or your problems so seriously. You are not that special, and everyone has their struggles. Listen more and speak less when you can. There's immense value in hearing other perspectives. Don't put limitations on yourself or let yourself be defined by what others say you are. Your potential is boundless; embrace it and pursue what truly resonates with you.

As for love and relationships, embrace your desires without hesitation. Life is too short not to explore. As Kacey Musgraves sings, "So, kiss lots of boys, kiss lots of girls, if that's what you're into…" Each connection, each moment shared, is part of your journey and contributes to your understanding of love. Follow your arrow, wherever it points; it's your life, and you deserve to live it authentically.

Ultimately, life is a tapestry woven from both joy and sorrow. Embrace it all. The highs and lows will shape you into who you are meant to be. So, step forward with courage, listen to your heart, and embrace the adventure that lies ahead.

With warmth and wisdom,

JES

Acknowledgements

Writing this book has been one of the most rewarding experiences of my life. None of it would have been possible without the people who supported me, the cities that welcomed me, or the strangers who traveled alongside me.

To my mom, thank you for giving me the gift of life. Your resilience, your dedication, and your love have been an inspiration to us all. I deeply admire the strong, and beautiful woman that you are. You are my role model.

To my dad, thank you for being my number-one cheerleader. Thank you for spending hours with me at the dinner table, reading every single thing I have ever written, and for always pushing me to be the best version of myself. You are my hero.

To my sister, Gianna, thank you for being my best friend. There is nobody like you in this world. You are my greatest love, and I will forever be proud of the woman you are.

To my brothers, Christian, Dominick, and Joseph, thank you for always keeping me in check and for loving me unconditionally. The world needs more strong, vulnerable, and compassionate men like you.

To all my friends and family, old and new, thank you for making this world a better place. You are proof that love knows no race, gender, or boundary. Thank you for giving me the gift of true, loyal, and honest friendship.

And finally, to any stranger who picked up this book: I hope you found a little bit of yourself in these pages. Thank you for supporting me.

www.ingramcontent.com/pod-product-compliance
Lightning Source LLC
Chambersburg PA
CBHW020227130626
46549CB00005B/1784